THE ART AND PRACTICE OF
GEOMANCY

THE ART AND PRACTICE OF
GEOMANCY

DIVINATION, MAGIC, AND EARTH
WISDOM OF THE RENAISSANCE

JOHN MICHAEL GREER

Foreword by Lon Milo DuQuette

WEISERBOOKS
San Francisco, CA / Newburyport, MA

First published in 2009 by
Red Wheel/Weiser, LLC
With offices at:
500 Third Street, Suite 230
San Francisco, CA 94107
www.redwheelweiser.com

ISBN: 978-1-57863-431-6
Library of Congress Cataloging-in-Publication Data is available upon request

Cover design by Dutton & Sherman Design
Text design by Donna Linden
Typeset in Aurea and Perpetua
Cover photographs: Earth illustration with intense rays and lightning © Argus/Shutterstock; Detail
in sky in photo of Michelangelo's David Statue in Florence, Italy © Elena Koulik/Shutterstock;
Authentic Physical Science Reckonings © Din/Shutterstock

Printed in the United States of America
TS
10 9 8 7 6 5 4 3 2 1
Text paper contains a minimum of 30% post-consumer-waste material.

CONTENTS

FOREWORD

"Seek earth, and heaven shall be added unto you!"
FRANCIS BENDICK[1]

"I love the earth."

The driver pretended he didn't hear me. From the moment he collected me at the airport in Bristol he allowed me to sit silently and be seduced by the charm and splendor of southwest England's green and pleasant pastures. Radstock, near Bath in Somerset was my destination. It was an area of the UK I had never visited before so I had no idea how long I would be able to savor my chauffeured religious experience.

Never had I seen so many shades of green in my life. It felt like I was living inside the swelling phrases of Blake's great national hymn, *Jerusalem*. A "countenance divine" did indeed shine forth upon these clouded hills. This was heaven on earth. No. This was heaven of earth.

I rolled down the window and inhaled the perfume of grass and soil warmed by the sun of mid July.

"I love the earth." I said again, this time under my breath.

I closed my eyes as if to take a snapshot of the moment, and was surprised to feel a tear burst over the lower lash of my right eye and coolly evaporate in the wind as it ran down my cheek. I assure you, in my jaded heart such sensitive moments are a rarity, and usually occur only in the fleeting seconds that follow the first and second sip of a late afternoon martini.[2] This day's rapture was most likely induced by the stress and debauchery of visiting five countries in seven days, and the realization that after this

---

1. Francis Bendick (Aleister Crowley). *The Earth.* The Equinox I (6). London, Fall 1911. Reprint. (York Beach, ME: Weiser Books, 1992). Supplement, p. 110.

2. Regrettably this pure bliss disappears around the third and fourth sip.

lecture I'd be returning home to my own bed. Whatever the cause, I was drunk on earth and wished the driver would stop the car so that I might stretch out in a field and soak the verdant ground with my tears of love.

The mental image of such an awkward and unseemly act immediately erased such daydreams, but for the first time in my life I realized deep down to the very core of my soul that the earth is a living, breathing, conscious being—an intelligence—a god(dess)—and that I was her child. My flesh her soil and mantle; my blood her rivers and streams and seas; my bones her stones and mountains; my heartbeat her molten core—my soul one with her soul.

What more palpable deity could humanity seek? What god more wonderful, more worthy of our awe, our gratitude, our prayers? We must certainly honor the sun as the ultimate source of light and life, but without earth to reflect the solar glory, without the earth and her manifold creatures Sol Invictus would remain eternally a god unworshipped.

Moreover, is not the earth herself sunlight made manifest? Earth is the climax of spirit's descent into matter—the magical lowest low that contains not only a spark of the highest high but everything else in between. Earth is the alchemical laboratory that transmutes light into life. Earth is the crowning finale of creation, and we are conscious creatures of the earth. As such you and I possess—we embody—the secret of spirit's return to godhead. As it is written in the *Emerald Tablet of Hermes,* "That *One Only Thing* (after God) is the father of all things in the universe. Its power is perfect, after it has been united to a spirituous earth."[3]

It is humanity's most ancient and self-evident fact of life—the sun is our father, the earth is our mother—and no matter how gender-neutral our culture may strive to become, it is the mother who first hears our cries. It is the mother who first responds to our needs. It is the mother who first answers our questions.

---

3. Manley P. Hall. *Lost Keys of Freemasonry* (Richmond, VA: Macoy, 1968), p. 96.

How ironic it is, then, that as we grow into headstrong youngsters we become less and less inclined to listen to the voice our mother. As hormone-blinded adolescents we embarrassedly shun her counsel and ridicule her prophetic warnings regarding the dire consequences of our shortsightedness and foolish behavior. As self-absorbed young adults we shut our minds completely to the possibility she could in any way understand what *our* life is like, or what is or is not in our best interest. It is not until we have reached a significant level maturity that we realize that we've been blessed since birth with our own personal omniscient oracle, one whose unconditional love for us is beyond all human comprehension.

For centuries the art of geomancy has been a proper and respectful means by which we, as children of the earth, purposefully affirm our recognition of the earth as a living intelligence capable of answering our questions. The techniques and apparatus have varied from century to century, culture to culture, but its oracular vocabulary of sixteen geomantic figures (each made up of one or two dots neatly stacked four high) have remained constant.

My introduction to the art of geomancy came in 1974 when I purchased a tiny book by Israel Regarde titled *A Practical Guide to Geomantic Divination*.[4] Its size was not intimidating and Regardie's straightforward (and seemingly sane) approach to the subject made it all sound very appealing to a wide-eyed young proto-magician. An added attraction was the fact that geomancy had been (at the turn of the 20th century) a favorite oracle of the members and adepts of the Golden Dawn—and oh! how I wanted to be like one of those Golden Dawn guys!

My expectations were high, perhaps too high, for this oracle of earth. I envisioned hairy little pipe-smoking gnomes popping up in my bedroom

---

4. Israel Regardie, *A Practical Guide to Geomantic Divination* (NY: Samuel Weiser, 1972).

temple to grumpily answer my questions and lead me to buried treasure in the back yard. What I found was what appeared to be an abbreviated (and not very exciting) variety of astrology. What does astrology have to do with an earth oracle? I was really hoping for something quick and easy I could do without having to study a bunch of other stuff. Geomancy was starting to look like work.

I nevertheless gritted my teeth and dug into that tiny book. In doing so I received my first (albeit remedial) lessons on the nature and basic meaning of the planets and signs of the zodiac, and of course, the names and meanings of the sixteen geomantic figures.

I have to confess that my first attempts to divine with geomancy were (from my perspective) abysmal failures. Not only did I not know enough about astrology to get a clear answer out of the chart that my dot juggling had generated, but my interpretations of what I thought I *did* understand turned out to be patently wrong (as future events proved in objective reality).

I asked (almost forced) Constance to give it a try. She has Taurus rising in her natal chart. She's got a green-thumb in the garden. She's the darling of all animals, insects, and flowers. I hoped perhaps her earthiness would be more in harmony with the art. She protested she didn't want to consult the "dirt oracle." Still, she was a good sport and reluctantly agreed to ask a question and proceeded to generate her "Four Mothers" by sixteen throws of tiny pebbles on the kitchen countertop. Her efforts generated the dreaded *Rubeus* in the first house. Ouch! That's bad! When that happens, the book told us we were supposed to abandon the operation and not try again for hours. It's the geomantic equivalent of the gypsy fortune-teller saying, "I see nooootheeeng! Go! Now! LEEEEEVE MY TENT!"

That did it for Constance; and pretty much for me too.

It would be a dozen years before I again developed any serious interest in the art of geomancy. Again it was a book, *The Oracle of Geomancy: Techniques of Earth Divination*[5] by Stephen Skinner, that triggered my interest. It was a clear and thorough overview of the basics and much longer

---

5. Stephen Skinner. *The Oracle of Geomancy: Techniques of Earth Divination* (Bridport, Dorset, San Leandro: Prism Press, 1986).

and more involved than Regardie's little book. Most importantly for me, it provided many helpful tables, examples, and ways one could arrive at simple answers to simple questions.

On board the geomancy train once again, I set to work to construct a "tray" specifically designed for geomantic divinations. Actually, it is a very shallow wooden box eighteen inches square and two inches deep. I lined the bottom with a thick layer of modeling clay. I eventually adorned the top and outer sides of the walls with the sixteen geomantic symbols and the names and sigils of the spirits along with their planetary and astrological symbols. With a pointed stick I marked out sixteen horizontal bands in the clay. During geomantic operations I use the same stick to "poke" the random marks within the bands to arrive at the initial Four Mother figures. I reserved part of the clay surface to accommodate the Mothers and the twelve other figures that they generate. The deep permanent lines on the surface of the clay make it possible to execute the figure-generating part operation entirely in clay without resorting to pencil and paper. I have to admit, it looks very magical and works marvelously well. The feeling that I am working directly with earth is powerful and unmistakable.

Finally, I had made peace with geomancy, and with the help of Skinner's book started cautiously to consult the "clay" for insights on personal issues that I determined were of an "earthy" nature. I also occasionally made myself available for friends and others who come to me for quick-and-dirty geomantic readings.

Still, I was not yet a passionate devotee of the art. The works of Regardie and Skinner helped me understand how the forces, energies, intelligences, and spirits of the planets and zodiac signs could "speak" through the element of earth. I was comfortable enough with the theory. But neither book had sparked the flame of true spiritual romance in my magical soul. I had not yet connected my heartfelt love of the earth to the cold manipulations of dots on a slab of clay.

The catalyst that would eventually provided this magical link for me is the book you are now reading. When the publisher asked me if I would write this foreword I was delighted to accept, and immediately asked them to send along the manuscript. I believe the author, John Michael Greer, to be one of the most knowledgeable and brilliant esoteric scholars alive today. He is also a friend and lodge brother who I see far too infrequently. I do not exaggerate; I could listen to John Michael Greer talk all day and all night. His wit and insight breathes life into the movements and personalities of the dusty esoteric past. It is as though he is the time-traveling custodian of the Library of Alexandria, or a medieval magician, or a Renaissance magus, transported through time to share with us the brilliance and relevance of our rich spiritual ancestry.

Something "clicked" in me when I read his historic vignettes in Chapter One. The simple, quiet charm of these little stories were for me the last alchemical ingredient in my long experiment with geomancy; the V.I.T.R.I.O.L. that dissolved way all that previously prevented me from uniting my heart with my mind. I devoured the rest of John's magnificent book with the passion of a teenager who has just discovered poetry. As I wrote him, "It is the greatest comment on geomancy ever written." I hope you will treasure it as much as I do.

"Glory be to the Earth and to the Sun and to the holy body and soul of Man; and glory be to Love and to the Father of Love, the secret Unity of things!

"Also thanksgiving in the Highest for the Gift of all these things, and for the maiden in whom all these things are found, for the holy body and soul of Man, and for the Sun, and for the Earth. AMEN."[6]

Lon Milo DuQuette
Costa Mesa, California
October 31, 2008

---

6. Francis Bendick (Aleister Crowley). *The Earth*. The Equinox 1 (6). London, Fall 1922. Reprint. (York Beach, ME: Weiser Books, 1992). Supplement, p. 110.

PART ONE

THE ART OF GEOMANCY

CHAPTER ONE

WHAT IS GEOMANCY?

The bright sun of an Italian afternoon poured through the window as the young man sat down. His bright garments and the sword at his side marked him as a member of the nobility, no small thing on that summer day in Padua in the early fourteenth century, but he seemed ill at ease as he considered the old man in a scholar's black cassock before him. He fumbled with words as he explained why he needed to peer into the secrets of the future, even if it meant risking his soul.

It concerned a young woman, of course—the daughter of another noble family in Padua. He loved her passionately, and a few whispered words from her lips in their one brief moment of privacy told him that she shared his feelings. Their families, however, stood on opposite sides in the bitter rivalries of the Paduan nobility. Was there any hope that he could marry his beloved?

The old scholar smiled. Over the years, as he practiced his secret art, he had heard this story more times than he could count. He rose from his seat, fetched a wax-coated wooden tablet and an iron stylus from its place on his desk, and handed both to the young man, telling him to mark sixteen lines of dots on the tablet, without counting how many dots he put in each line. Mystified, the young man nodded and closed his eyes, and the soft tapping of the stylus on wax sounded in the quiet room.

A few minutes later, the chart was finished:

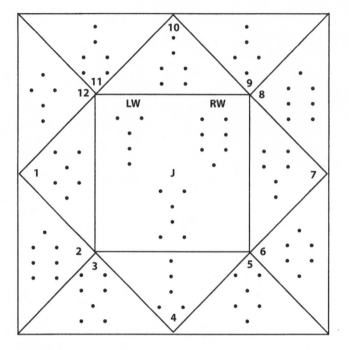

Figure 1-1 Pietro di Abano's Chart
In this chart the first house stands for the young man, and the seventh house for the woman he loves. The figure in the second and eighth house, Laetitia (happiness), makes a connection between them, and promises a successful result. This is confirmed by the Judge (the figure marked J in the diagram), which is Conjunctio (conjunction), the symbol of marriage.

The scholar tapped one place on the chart with his fingertip—the first house, he explained—and gestured to show how the figure next to it, Laetitia, "Happiness," also appeared on the other side of the chart, next to the seventh house of marriage. The figure in the first house, he said, was named Acquisitio, "Gain," and the figure in the seventh house was Fortuna Major, "The Greater Fortune"; he added them together and the result was the figure Conjunctio, "Union." The chart was very favorable, the scholar told the young man; if he broached the matter with his family and hers, the marriage would be brought about with ease.

The young man paid his fee and went away beaming. A few months later a messenger came to the scholar's door, gorgeously dressed in the livery of one of Padua's noble houses. He carried a letter inviting Pietro di Abano, doctor of philosophy at the University of Padua, to the wedding of the young man and his beloved.

• • •

Footfalls rang on the pavement outside, and the door creaked open, letting in a gust of damp evening air and a tall man dressed in the hunting costume fashionable among aristocrats in sixteenth-century France. "Monsieur Cattan!" he called out. "I have need of you."

Smiling, a dapper middle-aged man bowed out of a conversation at the other end of the hall and crossed to greet the newcomer warmly; the lord of Tays was a favorite of King Henri just then, and it would not do to keep him waiting. As Cattan had guessed, his lordship's need had to do with divination. This time it was a horse, a spirited roan offered for sale to his lordship. Was the beast worthy of the Tays stables?

A servant hurried away and returned with a quill pen, an inkpot, and several sheets of paper, wax tablets having gone out of fashion in the last century. Cattan seated himself before an ornate table at one side of the hall, paused in concentration, and cast the chart himself. A few minutes later he had an answer for his lordship.

"I am sorry to say the horse will disappoint you, Monsieur," Cattan told him. "A question such as this, as it pertains to horses or other great beasts, belongs to the twelfth house, here, and you see the figure Amissio, which means 'loss.' The Part of Fortune goes to the same house and shares in the same bad figure, and you see that the Judge is Carcer, 'prison,' another bad figure. Since Amissio passes nowhere else in the chart, the problem is in the foot, since the twelfth house governs that also. Have an experienced man check the beast's hooves and he will find some injury or deformity there."

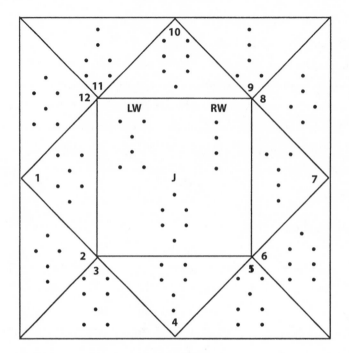

Figure 1-2 Christopher Cattan's Chart
In this chart the first house stands for the lord of Tays and the twelfth for the horse he hopes to buy. The figure in the twelfth house, Amissio (loss), is unfavorable, and so is the Judge, Carcer (prison). No positive factor intervenes in the chart, giving a definite negative answer.

The lord of Tays thanked him and went his way. Nothing was said about money, but a few days later one of his lordship's servants approached Cattan and handed him an elegant little silk purse. Its contents clinked delicately as it passed from hand to hand.

"And the horse?" Cattan asked.

"Lame in the left forefoot," the man told him. "Your familiar devil has good eyes." He hurried away. Cattan rolled his eyes, then glanced inside the purse and saw the comforting sheen of gold. Life at the king's court was far from cheap, and the money that came his way from geomancy was no small help in making ends meet.

• • •

Two men came to the gate of the Papal Vice-Legate's palace in Avignon; one of them, a young Englishman named Robert Fludd, gave his friend a nervous look. He had put on his best doublet and ruff, and the Vice-Legate's invitation was in his hand, but the temptation to hurry back to his rooms, pack his gear, and flee Avignon that night was a real one. The religious tensions between Catholic France and Protestant England were bad enough, but Fludd had also been accused of unlawful arts by some of the local Jesuits. If only he had kept his mouth shut about geomancy at that dinner party, he thought, or refused the young captain of the guards who begged him to cast a chart about that girl!

His friend, the apothecary Malceau, went through the gate with no sign of concern, and Fludd gathered up his courage and followed him. The guards at the palace door, resplendent in buff coats and polished steel, admitted the two young men without demur, and a servant waiting inside bowed and motioned for them to follow him down a long corridor.

A few minutes later Fludd knelt before the Vice-Legate and kissed his ring—a traditional courtesy he knew he could not afford to refuse. The Vice-Legate, a lean Italian whose pointed beard was the color of iron, considered him and said, "Signore Fludd, I gather that you are very well-versed in the art of geomancy. What do you truly think of that science?"

If he was to be turned over to the Inquisition, Fludd knew, that was how the process would start. Fumbling at first, he explained that he had practiced it for many years and believed it to be a truthful art whose foundations are hidden but in no way evil. The knowledge it brings, he said, comes from the interaction between the soul of the geomancer and the soul of the world, the *anima mundi*. The Vice-Legate asked more questions, precise as rapier thrusts, and Fludd warmed to his theme. He quoted the Bible and the classical philosophers to show that geomancy is natural, not supernatural, and that its powers are simply those of the human soul.

Finally the Vice-Legate smiled and held up a hand, interrupting Fludd. With a gesture, he led the young Englishman to a table, sat down, procured paper and a pen, and swiftly and skillfully cast a geomantic chart. He then interpreted it aloud with an assurance and expertise that showed Fludd he was in the presence of a master geomancer. "Those Jesuits who accused you," the Vice-Legate said finally, "they are fools. I cannot think of a single cardinal in all of Italy who has not had his horoscope cast, either by the astrological or the geomantic method." He rose. "But I have delayed our dinner. I hope you will do me the honor of sitting with me, Signore Fludd? It will be a pleasure to speak more of this most excellent art."

• • •

These vignettes from three of the classic geomantic texts of the Renaissance—Pietro di Abano's *Modo Judicandi Quaestiones (How to Interpret Divinations)*, Christopher Cattan's *Geomancie*, and Robert Fludd's *De Geomantia (On Geomancy)*—make a good introduction to the forgotten art of geomancy, one of the great branches of Renaissance occultism. The term "geomancy" these days sees use mostly as a label for Asian traditions dealing with the subtle aspects of space and placement, such as Chinese feng-shui and Hindu vaastu, or for speculations involving ley lines and Earth energies. Still, the word originally meant something quite different: an elegant, effective, and simple method of divination using sixteen abstract patterns formed of points, called geomantic figures.

During the centuries before the scientific revolution, when people needed information they could not get by ordinary means, geomancy was among the most widely used of all systems of divination across the Western world. Astrology had more prestige, but in the days before computers, casting a horoscope required plenty of paper or parchment—expensive commodities in the days before modern mass production—and a solid background in astronomy and spherical trigonometry. Not many people could afford that much education, and the cost of an astrological chart was accordingly high.

Tarot, in turn, was just another card game back then. Nobody thought of using cards for divination at all until the very end of the Renaissance, and it was the nineteenth century before tarot cards pulled ahead of the competition to become the world's most widely used divination deck. Palmistry

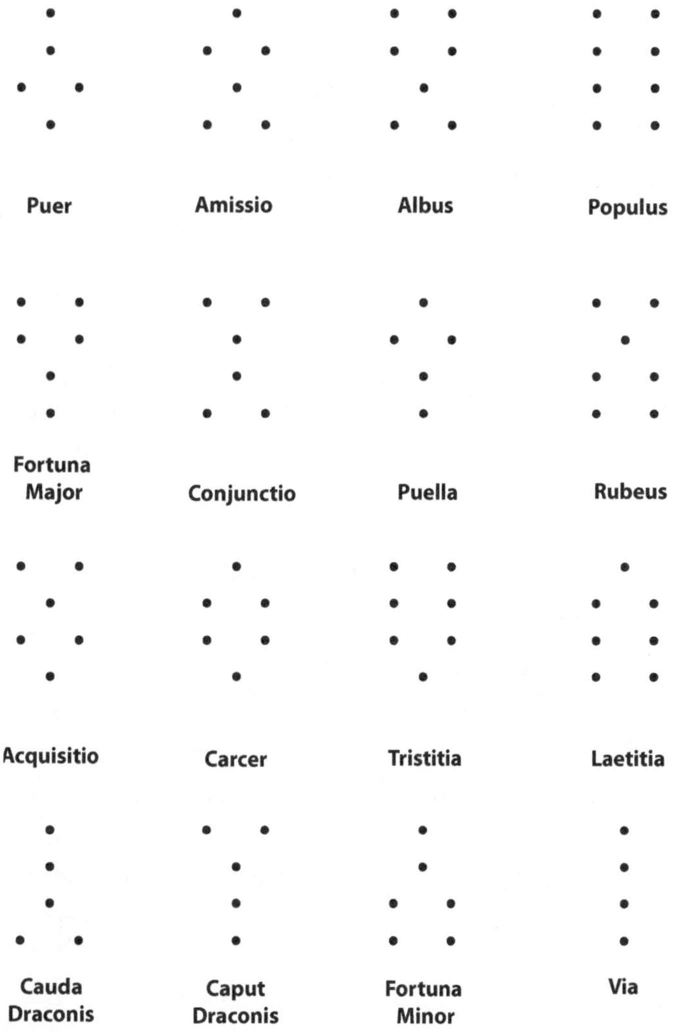

Puer	Amissio	Albus	Populus
Fortuna Major	Conjunctio	Puella	Rubeus
Acquisitio	Carcer	Tristitia	Laetitia
Cauda Draconis	Caput Draconis	Fortuna Minor	Via

Figure 1-3 The Geomantic Figures
These sixteen figures form the basic symbolic alphabet of geomancy.

was popular, but it's difficult for a palmist to answer more than a narrow range of questions about personality and destiny. The same problems faced metoscopy, another forgotten method of divination that reads faces the way a palmist reads hands, and most of the folk divination practices common in Renaissance culture were even more limited.

By comparison, geomancy has immense advantages. As a divination system, it is as flexible and informative as astrology, but much quicker, easier, and less expensive to practice. A geomantic chart takes only a few minutes to cast, it can be done on a napkin or even a square foot of bare soil, and anyone who can count, tell the difference between odd and even numbers, and work out the sums $1 + 1$, $1 + 2$, and $2 + 2$, knows all the mathematics needed for the purpose. Furthermore, like astrology but unlike most other divination systems known at that time, geomancy has deep roots in Renaissance occult philosophy, and its own traditions of meditation and ritual magic. It forms a complete system of divination, magic, and spiritual practice founded on an ancient vision of the Earth as a living, conscious entity.

The History of Geomancy

The geomancers of the Middle Ages and Renaissance would have been astonished that any of this needs to be explained at all. Less than four hundred years ago, practically everyone in the Western world knew about geomancy, and professional geomancers were as common in most communities as psychologists are today. Dozens of handbooks of geomancy saw print in the sixteenth and seventeenth centuries. These drew from an even larger collection of geomancy literature from the European Middle Ages, in which geomantic divination formed the core of a complete system of Earth wisdom with many practical and spiritual applications.

Although it was deeply rooted in medieval European culture, geomancy did not originate in Europe. The first European books on geomancy were translated from Arabic to Latin by Hugh of Santalla and

Gerard of Cremona in the early twelfth century, and historians agree that the Arabs had it long before that. Nobody's quite sure where the Arabs got it, but it first surfaced in North Africa sometime during the ninth century. One plausible theory suggests that it was an adaptation of older African divination systems, many of which use the same basic figures and interpret them in similar ways.

Geomancy had many names in the Arabic language; the most popular were *khatt al-raml*, "cutting the sand," and *'ilm al-raml*, "the science of sand," because most Arab geomancers used the desert sands as a convenient working surface. It became a part of everyday culture throughout the Arabic world. Diviners peering into the future appear in stories from *Arabian Nights*, for example, and to this day geomancers practicing the traditional Arabic form of the art can be found in marketplaces across the Muslim world, from Pakistan to Morocco.

The richly developed Arabic traditions of geomancy eventually moved north into the nations of Europe, part of a torrent of cultural treasures that helped end the Dark Ages and lay the foundations for the Renaissance. The same medieval European scholars who translated Greek philosophy and Muslim medical texts from Arabic to Latin turned their talents just as eagerly to handbooks of occultism, and geomancy was one of many arts that entered Europe in this way.

Once it arrived in Europe, geomancy spread just as rapidly as it had through the Muslim world and became an everyday part of the cultural scene. When the great Italian poet Dante Alighieri wanted a poetic simile for the rising sun, he could use the corresponding geomantic figure without having to explain it, as in Canto XIX of his *Purgatorio*, ". . . and the geomancer sees / His Greater Fortune up the east ascend," since every educated person in his time knew which geomantic figure was associated with each of the seven planets of astrology. In the same way, geomancers such as the three whose adventures opened this chapter could practice their art with only the most occasional interferences from church authorities. Geomancy was so widely practiced by people in all walks of life that nobody gave it a second thought.

Philosophers of Renaissance occultism, Robert Fludd among them, included in their books carefully reasoned arguments showing that geomancy was a natural art, drawing on the inborn powers of the human soul to glean information from the larger soul of the world. This reasoning was widely accepted all through the Renaissance, and guaranteed geomancy a place in the world. Not until modern scientific materialism seized control of the Western world's cultural imagination at the end of the seventeenth century, and imposed its own vision of a cosmos of dead matter in empty space, did geomancy drop out of popular culture into the shadowy underworld of occult lodges where the magical teachings of the Renaissance alone survived.

Even there, geomancy found few takers. The occult initiates who struggled to save this heritage of the Western world in those difficult years had to winnow down the traditions they guarded into forms compact enough that a single person could learn them quickly and pass them on to others just as quickly. Entire branches of occult practice dropped out of use as their guardians abandoned everything except what had to be saved, and geomancy was one of the systems that drew a short straw in this lottery of survival. By 1800 it endured as a living tradition only in the Muslim world and some parts of Africa. A few debased versions lingered on in the Western world as systems of fortune telling, but that was all.

This was still the case until the 1890s, when the founders of the Hermetic Order of the Golden Dawn, the occult lodge responsible for most of the modern revival of magic in the English-speaking world, stumbled upon it. Their source was the British Library's copy of one of the last major works of the Renaissance geomantic tradition, John Heydon's sprawling and difficult 800-page tome *Theomagia, or the Temple of Wisdome*, which was originally published in 1664. From this source, Golden Dawn Chief Samuel Mathers extracted a twenty-four-page summary of basic geomantic practice. That summary became a "knowledge lecture," one of the instructional papers that Golden Dawn initiates copied by hand and studied as they worked their way up the order's degrees of initiation.

Take 800 pages of anything and try to condense it into twenty-four pages, and it's a fair bet that quite a bit of knowledge won't make the transition. This is exactly what happened with geomancy. The Golden Dawn knowledge lecture provided a brief summary of the process of casting a chart, a few tables of canned meanings of the geomantic figures, and a very rough guide to interpreting the figures based on their position in the chart; in other words, a very basic introduction, rather than a detailed textbook of a complex divinatory art. To give the Golden Dawn its due, these papers were never meant to be more than an introduction, and would likely have been supplemented with more material from Heydon and other sources if the Golden Dawn had survived longer. The bitter political quarrels that blew the order apart between 1900 and 1903, however, made that a forlorn hope.

This left the knowledge lecture as the only readily available document on geomancy in the English language. Several writers in the years since then have tried to bring geomancy back into popularity, using the version of the art given in those twenty-four pages as the basis for their work. Not surprisingly, these have had a hard time attracting an audience. Would-be geomancers were taught how to cast a geomantic chart, then told to look up the results in a set of tables that offered such helpful comments as "Evil, except for bloodletting." Many people in the modern occult community ended up dismissing geomancy entirely as a crude method of divination with little value, or treated it as nothing more than one more hoop to jump through in the quest for magical initiation. Meanwhile, the full Renaissance tradition waited, locked away in Renaissance manuscripts few modern occultists knew enough Latin to read.

The irony, and it's not a small one, is that the Golden Dawn's attempt to revive geomancy turned into a barrier that prevented its revival as a complete system for more than a century. The twenty-four-page knowledge lecture has given far too many people an inaccurate idea of the scope and possibilities of the art. As a system of divination, geomancy is as subtle, intuitive, and informative as any oracle in the world.

Once a novice learns the sixteen figures and the basic methods of interpretation, canned answers from tables become irrelevant, because the meanings can be read right off the chart from the relationships between figures. Interpreted in this way, geomantic readings consistently give clear, straightforward answers to questions about the practical events of everyday life. While divination forms the core of traditional geomantic practice, the art of geomancy also includes methods of practical magic, meditation, and visionary experience, all based on a common view of a living, conscious Earth and a profound philosophy of nature.

The Soul of the World

Geomancy remains as relevant now as it ever was, not least because its perspectives point to dimensions of reality that today's society has forgotten, and desperately needs to relearn. To the diviners of earlier times, the entire world was a dance of meanings that could be read by the perceptive eye and interpreted by the attentive mind. When birds flew past from a particular direction, when the stars and planets assumed certain arrangements, or when the chance patterns of a geomantic divination gave rise to a specific set of figures and their interactions, some part of the great dance of the cosmos was brought into clearer view. All these events formed pages in what scholars and magicians of the Renaissance called the Book of Nature—a book that geomancers, among many others, studied with great care and learned how to read.

The old geomancers had no time for the modern notion that the world of nature is simply a passive collection of objects waiting for us to push our interpretations on them. From the geomancer's perspective, nature is an active, creative presence. Magicians and philosophers of the Middle Ages and Renaissance often spoke of two aspects of nature, using a convenient bit of Latin wordplay that relies on the fact that *natura*, "nature" in Latin, comes from a root meaning "to be born." One of these aspects they called *natura naturata*, "nature that is born": nature as a collection of things we can perceive with our outer senses, things that are born and live and pass away. The other they called *natura naturans*, "nature that gives birth": nature as a creative power that gives rise to everything that is born and lives and passes away. If *natura naturata* is the Book of Nature, then *natura naturans* is its author.

Closely related to this latter realization is the knowledge of the Earth as a living and conscious entity: not simply a mass of raw materials for our use, but an intelligent creature in whose vast body we live and move and have our being. Nowadays many people associate this idea with tribal cultures, or with scientists such as James Lovelock who have pointed out that the Earth does in fact behave like a single organism. Few remember that before the rise of modern materialist thought, the same concept had a central place in Western cultures as well.

The old magical philosophy of the West sees all living beings as unities formed of three aspects: *anima*, or soul, the aspect of consciousness and essence; *spiritus*, or life, the aspect of energy, imagery, and vitality; and *corpus*, or body, the aspect of material form. So alongside the *corpus mundi*, or body, of the world, the physical world of matter we experience with our senses, traditional lore places the *spiritus mundi*, the essential life-energy of the world, and the *anima mundi*, the soul of the world, its consciousness and innate intelligence.

It's in the anima mundi, the consciousness of the world, that the patterns perceived by geomancers take shape as rhythms in the interaction of the four magical elements: Earth, Water, Fire, and Air. Each of the geomantic figures, as explained in Chapters Two and Three of this book, represents a particular pattern of forces, with single and double dots representing active and passive elemental influences, respectively. These patterns echo outward through the spiritus mundi to become visible to our ordinary senses in the realm of the corpus mundi. A skilled geomancer can read these patterns in the dance of the geomantic figures before they reach manifestation, sense how those patterns will shape events, envision new patterns in the depths of meditation and scrying, and set those new patterns in motion with precisely chosen magical actions to bring events into a new state of balance.

The regular practice of divination is the key to learning this process. As you watch the dance of seemingly random events, use intuition to sense their meanings, and then compare the results to what actually happens, you can readily learn to use the subtle awareness of the old geomancers to make sense of the world. This is why divination formed the core of the old geomantic tradition, and other practices such as meditation and magic played a secondary role.

This marks one of the primary differences between Renaissance magic and its modern equivalents. In most of today's occult traditions, ritual magic takes the central role divination had in earlier times, and practitioners of modern magic spend much of their time learning how to raise power and direct it into their magical work. You won't find a word about raising power in Renaissance magical texts, however, because Renaissance occultists relied on the currents of power that exist around us at every moment. The shifting patterns made by those currents could be tracked in many ways, but geomancy—with its sixteen figures expressing the dance of elemental energies in the anima mundi—was one of the most valued.

This approach sets traditional geomantic practice apart from most modern magical paths in important ways. Still, the path of geomancy can be taken up and practiced successfully today. That path begins with the basic alphabet of geomancy—the symbolism and meanings of the sixteen geomantic figures—and proceeds from these through the essential skills of casting and interpreting geomantic divinations. Once these techniques have been mastered, geomantic methods of meditation, scrying, and ritual magic open new worlds to the geomancer, culminating in the summit of geomantic magic, the invocation of the guardian genius—the geomantic equivalent of the famous magical practice of the knowledge and conversation of the Holy Guardian Angel.

We'll explore these potentials later on in this book. First, it's necessary to learn the ABCs of geomancy—the symbolism and meaning of the sixteen geomantic figures.

CHAPTER TWO

THE ALPHABET OF GEOMANCY

The sixteen figures of geomancy may seem bare and abstract as the basis for a system of divination, especially when compared to the rich visual symbolism of tarot cards, say, or many of the other oracles popular in today's divination scene. Still, there's more to the geomantic figures than meets the eye; each one has a wealth of symbolism connected to it. Becoming familiar with those symbols is an unavoidable part of learning the art of geomancy.

Depending on how much you've worked with other divination systems or magical traditions, this learning process may seem heavy going at times. Still, there's no need to absorb it all at once—most students find that it's best to take plenty of time to learn the symbols, and focus on getting a general sense of the figures and their meanings, rather than trying to memorize everything right away. Plan on referring back to this chapter frequently as you learn the sixteen figures and begin working with them in divination and magic.

The Figures and the Four Elements

Different divination systems use larger or smaller sets of divinatory symbols, from the simple yes or no of a coin toss to the seventy-eight cards of a tarot deck and beyond. With only sixteen figures, the art of geomancy falls toward the simpler end of the spectrum. This is a source of strength in one sense, as it makes geomancy easier to learn and use than many other, more complex systems. When handled in a simplistic way, on the other hand, this limited range of symbols might also make geomancy less effective at communicating fine details or tracing out subtle connections.

Fortunately, the geomancers of the Middle Ages and Renaissance worked out many ways to find patterns and layers of meaning within the interplay of geomantic figures. As a result, geomantic divination has many different levels, reaching from basic approaches that provide broad general answers for the beginner, all the way up to subtle methods of analysis that make a geomantic reading as informative as any method of divination in the world. Much of the subtlety in geomantic divination comes in the process of setting up and interpreting the chart, which we'll explore in the lessons that follow. Part of the subtlety, however, comes from the inner structure of each of the sixteen figures.

Each geomantic figure consists of four lines of dots, with one or two dots in each line. The lines are traditionally called the head, neck, body, and feet of the figure, and they are assigned to the four elements of ancient magical philosophy: the head to Fire, the neck to Air, the body to Water, and the feet to Earth. This elemental meaning is the key to understanding the geomantic figures, and much else in the ancient magical conception of the world that underlies geomancy. The lines are shown below with Fortuna Major as an example.

* *	head line—Fire
* *	neck line—Air
*	body line—Water
*	feet line—Earth

Central to the old magical view of the world is a vision of the four elements as the basic patterns of everything in the world of our experience. Fire, Air, Water, and Earth in the geomantic sense aren't simply material substances, as some people think nowadays. Rather, they're patterns through which a single substance, the One Thing of the old alchemists, manifests in turn. When modern scientists describe a universe made up of energies, gases, liquids, and solids, they're using exactly the same idea in different words. Still, the old philosophy is much subtler than the new, and it doesn't limit its analysis to matter alone. Just as the universe of matter and energy expresses itself through these four patterns, so does the universe of the human mind; each of us has the fiery will, the airy mind, the watery emotions, and the earthy senses. In the same way, the four seasons, the four directions, and many other fourfold patterns reflect the dance of the four elements.

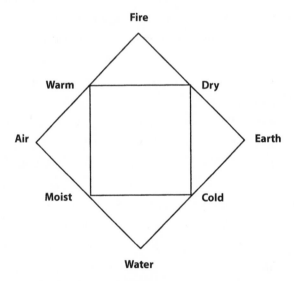

Figure 2-1 The Four Elements
This classic cosmological diagram shows the four elements as expressions of the four qualities of warmth, cold, moisture, and dryness.

Fire: Energy, activity, and purpose; corresponds to summer, noon, youth, and the will.

Air: Relation, response, and interaction; corresponds to spring, dawn, childhood, and the mind.

Water: Flow, receptivity, and change; corresponds to autumn, dusk, maturity, and the emotions.

Earth: Stability, form, and structure; corresponds to winter, midnight, old age, and the senses.

Each of the elements, in the magical vision of reality, combines with all the others to bring the world into being. Nothing in the world is made up of only one element. This is true even in the most material, matter-of-fact sense; a glass of water from the purest mountain stream contains fire in the form of latent heat, air in the form of dissolved gases, and earth in the form of dissolved minerals. The elements interweave in complex ways, but in the most general sense, an element can be *manifest*—that is, clearly present and active—or *latent*—that is, passive, dispersed, and hidden. In geomancy, a manifest element is represented by a single dot, and a latent element by a double dot.

In other words, look at the sixteen geomantic figures, and you're looking at a chart of the sixteen possible elemental states of anything. If all four elements are manifest, you have the geomantic figure Via; if all four elements are latent, you have the figure Populus. There are fourteen other possible states of elemental balance, each with its combination of latent and manifest elements. Take a moment to look back at the chart of geomantic figures in Figure 1-3, and see how each of them forms a chart of elemental relationships.

The manifest and latent elements in each figure define the *elemental structure* of the figure and provide the most basic level of meaning in a geomantic figure. It's valuable to study the elemental structure of each figure carefully, so that you can make sense of each figure at a glance. Your imagination is a valuable ally here. Imagine that each figure is actually made up of its manifest elements—Puer of Fire, Air, and Earth; Amissio of Fire and Water, and so on—and you'll quickly see how to read the structure and use it to make sense of the figure.

Symbolism of the Figures

The elemental structure is the framework of meaning for each figure, but plenty of other symbols, images, and ideas have been added to them by geomancers over the years. You don't need to memorize this additional information, but you should be familiar with and know how to make sense of it, because it can help you interpret the figures in divination and put them to work in meditation and magic.

Each of the figures, to begin with, has a *name*, and many have several other names as well. The names of the figures given in the last chapter, which are used throughout this book, are the most common ones, and are in Latin, the language of learning and scholarship in the Middle Ages and Renaissance. As with most things in geomancy, however, alternatives abound, and in many cases figures have alternative names that cast light on their wider meanings.

One of the four elements is considered to be the *inner element* of the figure. In every case but one—Populus, which has no manifest elements at all—the inner element is a manifest element, marked by a single dot. The inner element is also called the *ruling element*, and it stands for the elemental pattern that the figure expresses most intensely. Pay attention to the ruling elements in divination and you'll have a useful key to the way the events that are predicted or analyzed in a divination unfold in daily life. The inner elements of the figures are as follows:

Fire: Amissio, Laetitia, Cauda Draconis, Fortuna Minor

Air: Puer, Conjunctio, Rubeus, Acquisitio

Water: Albus, Populus, Puella, Via

Earth: Fortuna Major, Carcer, Tristitia, Caput Draconis

Each figure also has an *outer element*, which relates to the flow of elemental energies through the sixteen figures in their traditional sequence, which is given in Chapter Three. In a few cases this element is the same as the inner element, but usually it's different. The outer element shows how the figure expresses itself in the world around it, while the inner element shows what kind of power is in the figure itself. Fortuna Major, for example, has Fire as its outer element, which represents its power to reshape the world in a favorable way. The figure's inner element, however, is Earth, which means its power comes not from rushing around, but from establishing itself solidly and letting everything else move around it. The outer elements of the figures are as follows:

Fire: Puer, Fortuna Major, Acquisitio, Cauda Draconis

Air: Albus, Puella, Tristitia, Fortuna Minor

Water: Populus, Rubeus, Laetitia, Via

Earth: Amissio, Conjunctio, Carcer, Caput Draconis

Another important piece of symbolism is the division of the figures by *quality*. There are two qualities, mobile and stable, and they have a great deal to say in divinations about certain questions. In a question about some lost or stolen item, for example, a stable figure usually means the item will be recovered, while a mobile figure usually means it is gone for good. The qualities divide the figures as follows:

Mobile figures: Puer, Amissio, Conjunctio, Rubeus, Laetitia, Cauda Draconis, Fortuna Minor, Via

Stable figures: Albus, Populus, Fortuna Major, Puella, Acquisitio, Carcer, Tristitia, Caput Draconis

Each figure also has an *image* and a *keyword*. The image is simply a picture made from the points forming the figure, in a simplified "connect the dots" way. The keyword is a simple way of summing up the nature of the figure, and is there to help you learn the figures and their meanings.

In addition to the symbols already covered, quite a bit of the traditional symbolism used in geomancy actually comes from astrology. The influential sixteenth-century geomancer Christopher Cattan, in fact, called geomancy "the daughter of astrology" in his book on the subject. As the oldest continuously practiced form of divination in the Western world, astrology has been used as a resource for other systems of divination for many centuries; geomancy, palmistry, and Tarot, among many other divination methods, include astrological symbols. In the case of geomancy, the planets and signs of astrology also relate to subtle relationships between the heavens and the Earth central to the more advanced levels of geomantic practice. If you haven't studied astrology before and you have the opportunity to read a book or two on the subject, this can help you get a handle on the astrological side of geomantic symbolism.

The astrological side of geomancy begins by assigning a *planet* to each of the figures. In the days before telescopes, the sun, the moon, and five planets of the solar system—Mercury, Venus, Mars, Jupiter, and Saturn—were the only heavenly bodies that could be seen moving against the background of the stars. From the days of ancient Sumer, when the foundations of astrology were laid by astronomer-priests who watched the skies from atop mud-brick pyramids, these seven lights became the anchors for constellations of symbolism and meaning, and most traditional systems of divination include planetary lore. Fourteen of the sixteen geomantic figures are assigned to the seven planets. The two remaining figures, Caput Draconis and Cauda Draconis, are assigned to the nodes of the Moon, the two points in space where eclipses happen. The nodes get little attention in modern astrology, but the astrologers of the Middle Ages paid close attention to them, and treated them almost as planets in their own right. Geomancers found them equally useful as symbols for the potent energies of two of the most challenging figures of the sixteen. The planets and nodes relate to the figures as follows:

Saturn: Time, stability, contraction, limitation, and sorrow—
Carcer and Tristitia

Jupiter: Space, growth, expansiveness, abundance, and joy—
Acquisitio and Laetitia

Mars: Energy, will, transformation, and all masculine qualities—Puer and Rubeus

Sun: Balance, centrality, greatness, and success—Fortuna Major and Fortuna Minor

Venus: love, beauty, arts, the emotions, and all feminine
qualities—Amissio and Puella

Mercury: Communication, exchange, and the intellect—
Albus and Conjunctio

Moon: Receptivity, flow, the intuition, and cyclical change—
Populus and Via

Lunar Nodes: Radical change and disruption—Caput Draconis and Cauda Draconis

Another piece of symbolism from astrological sources is the *sign*
of the zodiac assigned to each figure. The zodiac is a band of twelve
constellations through which the sun, moon, and planets move when
seen from the viewpoint of the Earth. In very ancient times the constellations became markers for twelve equal sections of that band, and
each section gained its own wealth of symbolism and tradition. Geomancers in the Middle Ages and Renaissance used many diverse systems of assigning the figures to the signs of the zodiac. The one used in
this course, one of the most popular of them, follows the traditional
links between the planets and signs. Since there are sixteen figures and
only twelve signs, four signs each have two figures assigned to them.
The signs of the zodiac relate to the figures as follows:

Aries: The virile, energetic, and tactless Ram—Puer

Taurus: The stubborn, stable, and possessive Bull—Amissio

Gemini: The fickle, talkative, and mercurial Twins—Albus

Cancer: The sensitive, shy, and reflective Crab—Populus, Via

Leo: The proud, loyal, and ostentatious Lion—Fortuna Major, Fortuna Minor

Virgo: The prudent, methodical, and critical Virgin—Conjunctio, Caput Draconis

Libra: The elegant, adaptable, and unsteady Balance—Puella

Scorpio: The secretive, aggressive, and dangerous Scorpion—Rubeus

Sagittarius: The bold, honest, and impulsive Centaur—Acquisitio, Cauda Draconis

Capricorn: The solitary, austere, and patient Sea-Goat—Carcer

Aquarius: The idealistic, spiritual, and eccentric Water-Bearer—Tristitia

Pisces: The emotional, receptive, and ambivalent Fishes—Laetitia

The figures also relate to astrology by way of their *house relationships.* Astrological charts are divided into twelve houses, portions of the heavens assigned to different aspects of human life. One of the two basic forms of the geomantic chart, called the house chart, uses these same twelve divisions to help clarify the implications of a geomantic reading. Each figure is naturally favorable in certain houses and unfavorable in others, and these relationships play a role in interpreting the chart.

The signs of the Zodiac also determine the *house relationships* of the figures. In one of the two standard kinds of geomantic charts, the figures in the reading are distributed among twelve houses, corresponding to the twelve houses of astrology. Each house has a natural ruler among the signs, and each geomantic figure is strengthened when in the house of its natural ruler and weakened when in the opposite house.

The interface between geomancy and astrology also shows in another side of the figures' traditional symbolism. Each figure corresponds to a part of human *anatomy*, a traditional *body type*, and a *character type*, all of which have close echoes in old astrological sources. The body part is useful in divining questions dealing with health, while the body type and character type have a place in divinations where it's necessary to identify someone by appearance or personality—though it's important not to make the mistake of trying to do both at once! People with a personality that corresponds to one figure in particular, for example, can have a body type corresponding to any of the sixteen figures.

Related to these correspondences, but reaching deeper into the magical dimension of geomancy, is the traditional *color* or colors assigned to each figure. These can sometimes be useful in practical divination, but their main uses are in the art of scrying—a classic magical practice in which symbols such as the geomantic figures are used to open up awareness to the spiritus mundi—and the art of making geomantic sigils, talismans, and gamahes.

Finally, each figure has a *commentary* and a *divinatory meaning*. The commentary weaves together the symbolism of each figure and shows how the different symbols relate to one another, while the divinatory meaning sketches out the basic message the figure gives when it appears in a geomantic chart.

All these symbols may seem like so many abstractions at first glance. The best way to take them beyond that level, and experience them as part of the living dance of meaning expressed by each geomantic figure, is to study the way they relate to the individual figures themselves.

CHAPTER THREE

THE GEOMANTIC FIGURES

This chapter summarizes the characteristics of each of the sixteen geomantic figures, along with diagrams of their traditional patterns and the elements with which the patterns correspond. As mentioned already, the most important feature to note for divination purposes is the elemental structure of each figure, but familiarity with the symbols, images, and ideas included in the summary will help you in understanding all the dimensions of geomancy.

Puer (Boy)

Fire:	Active	•
Air:	Active	•
Water:	Passive	• •
Earth:	Active	•

Other names: Beardless, yellow, warrior, man, sword

Images: A sword; a male figure with exaggerated testicles

Keyword: Energy

Quality: Mobile

Planet: Mars

Sign: Aries

House relationships: Puer is strengthened in the first house and weakened in the seventh.

Outer element: Fire

Inner element: Air

Anatomy: The head

Body Type: Short, solidly built, and muscular, with a red face and small eyes. Skin color more brown or reddish than the person's ethnic background would suggest. Uneven teeth and, in men, a sparse beard.

Character Type: Rash, enthusiastic, and thoughtless, with plenty of energy and very little tact or self-control. The basic adolescent male personality, with self-assertion covering a great deal of insecurity and inexperience. People of this figure are prone to get into trouble by not thinking before they act.

Color: White, flecked with red

Commentary: Puer is a figure of male sexual energy, balancing the feminine figure Puella. Unstable and forceful, it represents conflict, sudden change, and transformation, with all the constructive and destructive aspects these imply. Its astrological symbolism, Mars, Aries, and Fire, carries forward this pattern of meaning. Its elemental lines and inner element, by contrast, point to a deeper level of interpretation: Puer possesses energy and purpose, interactions with others, and a material expression, but no receptive inner life. All the aspects of its nature are projected outward into the world of experience, as an act of creation or a source of delusion. Like a young warrior riding forth on a quest, it carries the spear of Fire, the sword of Air, and the disk or shield of Earth, but must seek the cup of Water elsewhere—an image that has more than a little to do with the inner meaning of the legendary quest for the Holy Grail.

Divinatory Meaning: Puer in a geomantic reading stands
for passionate energy, force, seeking, and sudden change.
In geomantic tradition, this figure is also associated with
justice. Whenever energy, enthusiasm, courage, and change
are desirable, Puer can be favorable, though even there it
can be problematic due to its unthinking nature. It is always
unfavorable in matters where stability, prudence, and maturity are advantages.

Amissio (Loss)

Fire:	Active	•
Air:	Passive	• •
Water:	Active	•
Earth:	Passive	• •

Other names: Grasping externally, outer wealth, something
escaped or lost

Image: A bag held mouth downward, letting the contents fall
out

Keyword: Loss

Quality: Mobile

Planet: Venus

Sign: Taurus

House relationships: Amissio is strengthened in the second
house and weakened in the eighth.

Outer element: Earth

Inner element: Fire

Anatomy: The neck and throat

Body Type: Middle height and large-boned body structure,
with a long neck, a large head, big shoulders and feet, and

a round face. The mouth is small and the eyes are attractive. Men of this figure tend to have facial hair, women have long and thick hair; in either case there may be a visible scar.

Character Type: Straightforward and sometimes tactless, quick to respond emotionally to any situation, deeply concerned with personal honor but not always honest.

Color: White, flecked with citrine (greenish yellow).

Commentary: Amissio is a figure of transience and loss, balancing Acquisitio's imagery of gain. Central to its meaning is a recognition of the hard truth that all things pass away. Its astrological symbols, Venus, Taurus, and Earth, point toward desire for material things as one of the classic examples of impermanence in human life; both the desire and the thing desired are certain to pass away in time, and so the experience of desire brings with it the certainty that the experience of loss will follow. Similarly, the elemental structure of the figure has Fire and Water alone; without Air to join them together or Earth to bring them into manifestation, these two opposed elements fly apart, and any contact between them is impermanent and without result.

Divinatory meaning: In a geomantic reading Amissio stands for loss in every sense, positive or negative, from losing your heart to losing your money. It often represents something outside one's grasp. Traditionally this is also a figure of generosity. It is favorable in any matter where loss is what you desire; this includes such things as love and sexuality (losing your heart), recovery from sickness (losing your illness), facing things you fear (losing your fear), and getting out of difficult situations (losing your problems). It is unfavorable whenever you hope to gain something from the situation.

Albus (White)

Fire:	Passive	• •
Air:	Passive	• •
Water:	Active	•
Earth:	Passive	• •

Other names: None

Image: A goblet set upright

Keyword: Peace

Quality: Stable

Planet: Mercury

Sign: Gemini

House relationships: Albus is strengthened in the third house and weakened in the ninth.

Outer element: Air

Inner element: Water

Anatomy: The shoulders and lungs

Body Type: Apple-shaped—that is, larger above the waist than below it—and medium height. The head is large, the face round, the eyes relatively small. Men of this figure often have a thick beard.

Character Type: Peaceful, kind, and loving, with a shy streak. People of this figure tend to make friends easily but keep few of them, and often spend money more freely than they can afford.

Color: Brilliant white, flecked with red

Commentary: Albus is a figure of peace and detachment, balancing the passionate figure Rubeus. Its astrological symbols, Mercury, Gemini, and Air, point to the way in which detachment has most often expressed itself in the Western world—the way of the intellect, which moves away from direct experience into abstract ideas. More deeply, though, Albus is a figure of Water, which is its only active line and also its inner element; it represents awareness caught up wholly in its own inner life and turned away from the action in the outer world of experience. In its highest form, this inward focus can lead the attentive mind to transcendence by the ways of mysticism, but it can also become a retreat from life that ends in sterility, isolation, and madness.

Divinatory meaning: Albus in a geomantic chart stands for peace, wisdom, and purity; it is generally a favorable figure, but often weak, and where it occurs, you may need to seek help from other people. It is traditionally a figure of chastity. Albus favors quiet progress and the use of intelligence, and is favorable in most business and financial questions; it is also favorable for beginnings. It is unfavorable in matters requiring courage and energy, or in any situation involving conflict or disruptive change.

Populus (People)

Fire:	Passive	• •
Air:	Passive	• •
Water:	Passive	• •
Earth:	Passive	• •

Other names: Congregation, multitude, double path

Image: A crowd

Keyword: Stability

Quality: Stable

Planet: Moon

Sign: Cancer

House relationships: Populus is strengthened in the fourth house and weakened in the tenth.

Outer element: Water

Inner element: Water

Anatomy: The breasts and midriff

Body Type: Tall and relatively thin, with narrow hips and a long face, large teeth, and skin darker than the person's ethnic background would normally suggest. People of this figure often have a mark or blemish near one eye, or one eye of a different size or color than another. The face is often more attractive than the body. Men of this figure commonly have a thick beard.

Character Type: People of this figure are passive and receptive, taking on the characteristics of those around them, and are happiest when in the company of friends. Their emotions are stronger than their intellect. An unexpected wandering streak makes them fond of travel and discontented when they have to remain in one place for too long.

Color: Sea green or dark russet brown

Commentary: Populus is a figure of dispersal and multiplicity, balancing the focused movement of Via. Its astrological symbols, the Moon, Cancer, and Water, are all images of passivity, reflection, and indirect action; they represent patterns of experience that have no direction or focus of their own, but simply respond to energies coming from outside. The elemental structure of the figure shows all four elements as passive and latent, but the receptive nature of Water comes closest to expressing the figure's nature in elemental terms. Like a crowd, Populus has no particular motion or direction until it receives the energy of another figure. Its stability is a function of sheer inertia, rather than of any special strength of its own.

Divinatory meaning: Populus in a geomantic chart represents a gathering or assembly of people, or a large amount of anything else. A passive figure that takes on the qualities of the figures that interact with it, Populus tends to be fortunate with fortunate figures and unfortunate with unfortunate ones. Still, it is usually favorable in matters that benefit from quiet reflection, and unfavorable in matters demanding focused action.

Fortuna Major (Greater Fortune)

Fire:	Passive	• •
Air:	Passive	• •
Water:	Active	•
Earth:	Active	•

Other names: Inward fortune, protection going in, greater omen, inside or hidden help

Image: A valley through which a river flows

Keyword: Power

Quality: Stable

Planet: Sun

Sign: Leo

House relationships: Fortuna Major is strengthened in the fifth house and weakened in the eleventh.

Outer element: Fire

Inner element: Earth

Anatomy: The heart and chest

Body Type: Medium height and slender build; the legs are often asymmetrical, with one longer or thicker than the other. Skin color tends to be more yellow than the person's ethnic background would normally suggest. A round face, attractive teeth, and large luminous eyes.

Character Type: Generous, honest, trustworthy, and fair, with an ambitious streak but a modest demeanor and an easy manner. Fond of spending money.

Colors: Green, yellow, or gold

Commentary: Fortuna Major is a figure of inner strength and resulting success, balancing the outer strength of Fortuna Minor. Its astrological symbols, the Sun, Leo, and Fire, are standard metaphorical images for strength and victory, but its elemental structure leads in some unexpected directions. Fire and Air are passive in this figure, with Water and Earth active, and the inner element is Earth; like the valley that is its image, Fortuna Major represents a natural shape of events that brings success without apparent effort. Though we too often tend to think of success as a matter of vigorous action and struggle, real success comes about because our inner life is reflected in our outer circumstances (as it always is, for good or ill) without any conscious effort at all. This is one of the central secrets of magic.

Divinatory meaning: Fortuna Major in a geomantic chart foretells great good fortune, although the way there may be difficult at times. It is a figure of power and success that unfolds naturally rather than having to be forced, and is especially favorable whenever the querent desires to win something. It often predicts a difficult beginning leading to a very good result. Traditionally it is a figure of nobility. Fortuna Major is favorable for nearly all questions except those involving escaping from a difficult situation; the Fortuna Major response to difficulty is to press ahead, and make lemonade out of life's lemons.

Conjunctio (Conjunction)

Fire:	Passive	• •
Air:	Active	•
Water:	Active	•
Earth:	Passive	• •

Other names: Association, gathering together

Image: A crossroads

Keyword: Interaction

Quality: Mobile

Planet: Mercury

Sign: Virgo

House relationships: Conjunctio is strengthened in the sixth house and weakened in the twelfth.

Outer element: Earth

Inner element: Air

Anatomy: The intestines and belly

Body Type: Very attractive, with a slender, delicate build and medium height. The face is long and beautiful, with a slender nose and attractive eyes. The thighs are thin. Men of this figure who have beards keep them short and neatly trimmed.

Character Type: Intelligent and talkative, fond of luxuries, and unconcerned with issues of honesty and legality. People of this figure have many friends and tend to spend more money than they earn.

Colors: Purple or pale gray, sometimes black speckled with blue

Commentary: Conjunctio is a figure of contact and union, balancing the isolated and limited figure Carcer. It represents the union of opposites on all levels and the resulting potentials for change. Here the astrological symbolism of Mercury, Virgo, and Earth ties into ancient magical images of fertility, and the elemental structure is open to energy in the Fire line and to manifestation in the line of Earth. Air and Water, the active elements in this figure, are thought of in magical philosophy as middle realms uniting the two ends of the elemental spectrum; Air, the inner element of this figure, also has a role here as a symbol of interaction. Like a crossroads, Conjunctio forms a context in which movement can lead in unexpected directions, and bring energies and people on highly different trajectories into interaction.

Divinatory meaning: Conjunctio in a geomantic chart shows the presence of a combination of forces. It tends to be favorable or unfavorable depending on other figures and circumstances, but is reliably favorable in any question about recovering things lost or stolen. It is traditionally a figure of temperance. It is favorable for matters in which things need to come into contact, and unfavorable for any situation that calls for solitude, separation, and clarification.

Puella (Girl)

Fire:	Active	•
Air:	Passive	• •
Water:	Active	•
Earth:	Active	•

Other names: Beauty, purity

Image: A mirror; a female figure with exaggerated breasts

Keyword: Harmony

Quality: Stable

Planet: Venus

Sign: Libra

House relationships: Puella is strengthened in the seventh house and weakened in the first.

Outer element: Air

Inner element: Water

Anatomy: The kidneys and lower back

Body Type: Attractive, with medium height and a soft, somewhat plump body. The neck is long, the face round, the mouth small, the eyebrows and eyes attractive, and the shoulders large. People of this figure sing well and speak in an attractive voice.

Character Type: Passionate and highly emotional, with a quick temper. People of this figure are intensely conscious of their appearance, and fall in and out of love easily.

Colors: White, flecked with green

Commentary: Puella is a figure of female sexual energy, balancing the masculine figure Puer. Puella is balanced and harmonious, but ambivalent. Its astrological symbols, Venus, Libra, and Air, suggest polar opposites held together in harmony and interaction by way of love, while its ruling inner element Water suggests that its energies are turned within, into a reflective inner life. The elemental structure is the key to this figure; with purpose and energy, inner receptivity, and the stability of a material basis, Puella lacks only relationship and interaction to be complete. It seeks to unite with others, where its opposite Puer seeks only to be received—a distinction that has more than a little to say about the complexity of relationships between the sexes.

Divinatory meaning: Puella in a geomantic reading stands for harmony and happiness that may not last indefinitely; it is a favorable figure in most questions, but fickle. It is especially favorable for questions involving love and friendship, and brings a positive answer to any question involving short-term happiness. Because of its fickleness, however, it is unfavorable in any situation where permanence is wanted.

Rubeus (Red)

Fire:	Passive	• •
Air:	Active	•
Water:	Passive	• •
Earth:	Passive	• •

Other names: Burning, danger

Image: A goblet turned upside down

Keyword: Passion

Quality: Mobile

Planet: Mars

Sign: Scorpio

House relationships: Rubeus is strengthened in the eighth house and weak in the second.

Outer element: Water

Inner element: Air

Anatomy: The genitals and reproductive system

Body Type: Strong and muscular, with skin more reddish or brown than the person's ethnic background would normally suggest. The face is rugged and often has red spots or boils. People of this figure have deep voices and hair that refuses to stay neat. Men of this figure have sparse beards.

Character Type: Hot-tempered, passionate, and troublesome, fond of partying, fighting, and lovemaking. Addictions to alcohol or drugs are common in people of this figure. Rubeus definitely means a walk on the wild side!

Colors: Red, flecked or streaked with brown.

Commentary: Rubeus is a figure of passion and involvement in life, balancing the abstract detachment of Albus. Its astrological symbols, Mars, Scorpio, and Water, are the standard images of passionate energy in the symbolic language of the heavens. Its inner element and the one active part of its elemental structure, however, are both Air. The lesson here is that passionate involvement in the world comes from focusing on how we relate to others and to the world itself. At its worst, this too easily becomes a blind intoxication with appearances, but it also has the potential to open the way to a joyous participation in the experience of life.

Divinatory meaning: Rubeus in a geomantic chart is a challenging figure that stands for passion, pleasure, fierceness, and violence. Old books on geomancy describe it as "good in all that is evil and evil in all that is good." It is unfavorable in most situations, but favorable in questions involving sexuality, intoxicants, and violence.

Acquisitio (Gain)

Fire:	Passive	• •
Air:	Active	•
Water:	Passive	• •
Earth:	Acive	•

Other names: Grasping internally, inner wealth, something gained or picked up

Image: A bag held mouth upward, as though to take something in

Keyword: Gain

Quality: Stable

Planet: Jupiter

Sign: Sagittarius

House relationships: Acquisitio is strengthened in the ninth house and weakened in the third.

Outer element: Fire

Inner element: Air

Anatomy: The hips and thighs

Body Type: Short but strongly built, with a full chest and skin color darker than the person's ethnic background would normally suggest. Arms and legs are short, and the neck is short and thick. The face is round, head large, mouth and eyes small.

Character Type: Fierce and passionate, with an insatiable gusto for life but an equally intense sense of fairness and justice.

Colors: Red, yellow, or green

Commentary: Acquisitio is a figure of gain and success, balancing the imagery of loss in Amissio. In its astrological symbolism, Jupiter is the traditional planet of good fortune, while Sagittarius and Fire represent energy directed toward goals. Its inner element and elemental structure stress that real gain of any kind exists only in a web of interaction, and seeks productive manifestation; all the money in the world is useless if no one will accept it in exchange, or if it simply piles up untouched. The elemental structure also suggests the far from minor point that material gain, despite all its potential for interaction and material wealth, does not necessarily add up to the fulfillment of one's desires or the deepening of one's inner life.

Divinatory meaning: Acquisitio in a geomantic reading foretells success, profit, and gain, and often means that something desired is within your grasp. Traditionally, Acquisitio is a figure of prudence. It represents gain in every sense, and favors any situation where gaining something is desired. It is unfavorable whenever loss is desired, such as illness, facing things you fear, and getting out of difficult situations.

Carcer (Prison)

Fire:	Active	•
Air:	Passive	• •
Water:	Passive	• •
Earth:	Acive	•

Other names: Constricted, lock

Image: An enclosure

Keyword: Isolation

Quality: Stable

Planet: Saturn

Sign: Capricorn

House relationships: Carcer is strengthened in the tenth house and weakened in the fourth.

Outer element: Earth

Inner element: Earth

Anatomy: The knees and lower legs

Body Type: Medium height and a wiry, sinewy build, with a long neck, small ears and mouth, and eyes that tend to look downward all the time. People of this figure often have strong muscular tensions, especially in the shoulders and around the mouth.

Character Type: Timid, especially about money and property, but stubborn. People of this figure tend to save more than they spend, and are fussy about their appearance.

Colors: White, russet, or dun (pale brown)

Commentary: Carcer is a figure of restriction and isolation, balancing the open and interactive nature of Conjunctio. This pattern of meanings has two sides, for restriction can be a source of strength and focus as well as a limitation. This is shown in its astrological symbolism, for Saturn, Capricorn, and Earth establish an imagery of rigidity and fixation, but also one of energy expended in productive work. The elemental structure develops the same theme; Fire and Earth represent energy and material expression, but they also remain at the two ends of the elemental spectrum, unable to come into contact with each other because neither of the middle elements are there to bridge the gap.

Divinatory meaning: Carcer in a geomantic chart represents solidity, restriction, binding, or even imprisonment. It always portends delay. In financial questions, it can stand for greed. It is unfavorable in most questions, but favors anything involving stability, security, and isolation.

Tristitia (Sorrow)

Fire:	Passive	• •
Air:	Passive	• •
Water:	Passive	• •
Earth:	Active	•

Other names: Crosswise, diminished, accursed, head down, fallen tower, cross

Image: A pit, a stake driven downward

Keyword: Sorrow

Quality: Stable

Planet: Saturn

Sign: Aquarius

House relationships: Tristitia is strengthened in the eleventh house and weakened in the fifth.

Outer element: Air

Inner element: Earth

Anatomy: The ankles

Body Type: Tall and thin, with knobby joints, large feet, and darker skin than the person's ethnic background would normally suggest. The face is long, the teeth large, and the hair rough and unkempt.

Character Type: Unconventional and idealistic, unconcerned with social expectations, and prone to dishonesty. People of this figure have quick tempers and carry grudges for a long time.

Colors: Tawny or sky blue

Commentary: Tristitia is a figure of sorrow and difficulty, balancing the joyous symbolism of Laetitia. Its astrological symbolism is complex; Saturn has traditional links to ideas of pain and trouble, and these are reinforced by turbulent Air, but Aquarius carries meanings of creativity and benevolence that may seem hard to relate to the symbolism of Saturn. The elemental structure and inner element stress Earth to the exclusion of all else, and this may also seem hard to connect to the other astrological symbols. The deeper level of meaning where these paradoxes resolve is simply that suffering is the one sure source of wisdom; too often, it's only when we are "stuck," caught up in a painful situation we do not know how to resolve, that we learn to face the world in more creative ways.

Divinatory meaning: In a geomantic reading, Tristitia stands for any downward movement. Lowered spirits (sorrow), lowered vitality (illness), and lowered expectations (failure) all fall within its ambit, though it can also mean stability and solidity, the sinking of roots deep into the ground. Unfavorable in most matters, it is favorable for questions involving stability and patience. It is very favorable in all questions dealing with building and the Earth, where its quality of "stuckness" or permanence is wanted, and for any situation in which a secret needs to be kept.

Laetitia (Joy)

Fire:	Active	•
Air:	Passive	• •
Water:	Passive	• •
Earth:	Passive	• •

Other names: Bearded, laughing, singing, high tower, head lifted, candelabrum, high mountain

Image: A tower

Keyword: Joy

Quality: Mobile

Planet: Jupiter

Sign: Pisces

House relationships: Laetitia is strengthened in the twelfth house and weakened in the sixth.

Outer element: Water

Inner element: Fire

Anatomy: The feet

Body Type: Tall and muscular, with large hands, feet, facial features, and forehead. People of this figure usually have rough and unruly hair, and a puppyish, ungainly air.

Character Type: Honest and good-natured, with a strong quality of innocence that can sometimes express itself as clueless folly. People of this figure often have strong and deeply held religious beliefs.

Colors: Glittering pale green

Commentary: Laetitia is a figure of joy, balancing the harsh symbolism of Tristitia. It represents happiness of every kind and level, from the most momentary of passing pleasures to the highest reaches of human experience. In its astrological symbolism, Jupiter has its usual role as the planet of good fortune, and watery Pisces and the outer element, Water, represent the emotional life, the context in which joy is usually experienced. The inner element and the elemental structure generally, however, stress the role of energy in the attainment of happiness; it is by way of the free flow of creative force, in ourselves as in the universe, that joy comes into being.

Divinatory meaning: Laetitia in a geomantic reading is a very positive figure representing any form of ascent. It means upward movement, which is favorable in a querent's career (success), emotional state (happiness), or vitality (health). It is traditionally a figure of fortitude, and is thus favorable in most questions, but is unfavorable for any question in which stability and deep roots are needed, and very unfavorable when a secret needs to be kept.

Cauda Draconis (Tail of the Dragon)

Fire:	Active	•
Air:	Active	•
Water:	Active	•
Earth:	Passive	• •

Other names: Outer threshold, threshold going out, lower boundary, stepping outside

Image: A doorway with footprints leading away from it

Keyword: Ending

Quality: Mobile

Planet: South node of the Moon

Sign: Sagittarius

House relationships: Cauda Draconis is strengthened in the ninth house and weakened in the third.

Outer element: Fire

Inner element: Fire

Anatomy: The left arm

Body Type: A long, thin body more attractive from behind than in front, with long-fingered hands. The face is long and lean, with a strong face and a large nose.

Character Type: Corrupt, dangerous, destructive, and self-destructive, without scruples or conscience. People of this figure are obsessed with their own perceived needs and wants, and pursue them without regard for anyone or anything else.

Colors: Green, white, dark crimson, or pale tawny brown

Commentary: Cauda Draconis is a symbol of endings and completions, balancing the symbolism of beginnings in Caput Draconis. Its astrological symbolism is that of the south or descending node of the Moon—the point at which the Moon crosses the Sun's path to go into the southern heavens. This point has some of the same symbolism as Mars and Saturn, the two malefics or negative forces in traditional astrology, and so Cauda Draconis symbolizes disruptions, losses, and endings. Its inner and outer elements are both Fire; the elemental structure, which lacks only Earth, suggests a situation nearing completion and thus ripe for radical change.

Divinatory meaning: In a geomantic reading, Cauda Draconis represents ending, completion, and letting go of the past. A figure with a complex message, it brings good with evil and evil with good, but is traditionally a figure of generosity. It is favorable in any situation where something is coming to an end, but unfavorable for most other questions.

Caput Draconis (Head of the Dragon)

Fire:	Passive	• •
Air:	Active	•
Water:	Active	•
Earth:	Active	•

Other names: Inner threshold, threshold coming in, upper boundary, high tree, upright staff, stepping inside

Image: A doorway with footprints leading toward it

Keyword: Beginning

Quality: Stable

Planet: North node of the Moon

Sign: Virgo

House relationships: Caput Draconis is strengthened in the sixth house and weakened in the twelfth.

Outer element: Earth

Inner element: Earth

Anatomy: The right arm

Body Type: Medium height and slender build, with an attractive and expressive face. People indicated by this figure have abundant hair and prominent facial features.

Character Type: Calm, trustworthy, and good-natured. An instinctive kindness is one of the most striking features of people of this figure.

Colors: White, flecked with citrine

Commentary: Caput Draconis is a figure of opportunities and beginnings, balancing Cauda Draconis's symbolism of endings. As the geomantic equivalent of the north or ascending node of the Moon, Caput Draconis shares much of the same focus on drastic change as Cauda, but the north node—the point at which the Moon crosses the Sun's path into the northern heavens—shares some of the symbolism of Venus and Jupiter, the two benefics or positive forces in traditional astrology. This figure thus represents change for the better, and is a particularly positive sign for beginnings. Earth, which is both its inner and outer element, and its elemental structure generally suggest fertile ground, needing only the energy of seed and sunlight; still, much depends on the seed that is planted there.

Divinatory meaning: In a geomantic reading, Caput Draconis represents beginnings and new possibilities. It tends to vary in meaning with its company, becoming more favorable with favorable figures and more unfavorable with unfavorable ones, but it often foretells a good result with some difficulty at the beginning. Caput Draconis is favorable in all matters having to do with beginnings, and unfavorable in questions where ending something is desirable.

Fortuna Minor (Lesser Fortune)

Fire:	Active	•
Air:	Active	•
Water:	Passive	• •
Earth:	Passive	• •

Other names: Outward fortune, protection going out, lesser omen, outside or apparent help

Image: A mountain with a staff atop it

Keyword: Swiftness

Quality: Mobile

Planet: Sun

Sign: Leo

House relationships: Fortuna Minor is strengthened in the fifth house and weakened in the eleventh.

Outer element: Air

Inner element: Fire

Anatomy: The spine

Body Type: Medium height and heavy build, with strong bones. The face is round and pale, the nose and forehead large, and the eyes dark. People of this figure have thick, rough, unkempt hair, and men tend to have beards of moderate length.

Character Type: Bold, proud, and presumptuous, with a streak of insecurity and humility underneath the bravado, and a great deal of generosity and a strong sense of honor.

Colors: Gold or yellow

Commentary: Fortuna Minor is a figure of outer strength and success, balancing the inner strength of Fortuna Major. These two figures have the same astrological symbolism but the opposite elemental structure; they represent the same kind of experience—success—but have sharply different sources. Fortuna Minor represents success that is brought about by outside help or circumstances, rather than by the innate strength symbolized by Fortuna Major. Easily gained, the success of Fortuna Minor is just as easily lost, and it produces the best results in situations where rapid change is expected or desired. These factors are echoed in the symbolism by an unexpected shift in the outer element; Leo is a fiery sign, but Fortuna Minor is usually given the outer element of Air, representing the role of outside help in this figure as well as the instability of the results.

Divinatory meaning: Fortuna Minor in a geomantic reading represents unstable success. It is traditionally a figure of inconstancy, and also of generosity, and warns that what you gain may not stay with you for long. It is very favorable whenever you want to proceed quickly, and unfavorable for matters in which fickleness or instability is a problem.

Via (Way)

Fire:	Active	•
Air:	Active	•
Water:	Active	•
Earth:	Active	•

Other names: Wayfarer, candle, journey

Image: A road

Keyword: Change

Quality: Mobile

Planet: Moon

Sign: Cancer

House relationships: Via is strengthened in the fourth house and weakened in the tenth.

Outer element: Water

Inner element: Water

Anatomy: The stomach

Body Type: Pear shaped (that is, larger below the waist than above it) and medium height, with a tendency to put on weight and sweat easily. People of this figure tend toward pale skin, round faces, and small teeth. One eye may be a different color than the other, or may have a birthmark or blemish nearby.

Character Type: Patient and silent, with a deep inner life that rarely shows on the surface. Slow to anger, but once angered, equally slow to forgive. Fond of travel and moving from place to place.

Colors: White, flecked with blue

Commentary: Via is a figure of directed movement and change, balancing the diffuse and formless stability of Populus. These two figures, like Fortuna Major and Fortuna Minor, share the same astrological symbolism but have opposite elemental structures. Here, however, the opposition is between complete passivity and complete activity. With all four elements active, Via represents the elements in a constant state of change, each giving way to the next in an endless cycle. There is, however, a certain passive, reflective quality shared by these most opposite of figures. Despite the common figure of speech, roads actually go nowhere; it is the travelers who follow them that go somewhere, leaving more of the road behind with each step.

Divinatory meaning: Via in a geomantic reading represents change in all its forms, and favors all questions in which change is an advantage. It is favorable for journeys of all kinds, real and metaphorical, but unfavorable whenever leaving things unchanged is desirable.

PART TWO

GEOMANTIC DIVINATION

CHAPTER FOUR

CASTING A GEOMANTIC READING

As explained in Chapter One, the art of divination depends on subtle links between human consciousness and the anima mundi, the consciousness of the world itself. Even in the Middle Ages and Renaissance, when humanity had not completely closed itself off from the living world behind walls of intellectual abstraction, opening up these subtle links required a certain degree of patience and specific disciplines, and that remains true today. Certain practical issues, including the choice of geomantic tools, also need to be settled before geomancy can be practiced effectively, and so does the surprisingly difficult business of choosing a question for divination that will get you the information you need. All these issues, as well as the much simpler process of casting a geomantic chart, will be covered in this chapter.

Places, Times, and Conditions for Divination

First of all, it's worth taking a moment to discuss the basic practical requirements for geomantic divination. These are very simple. A quiet place to sit, a pen or pencil, and some blank paper make up the basic kit. You may wish to add special tools for casting the four "Mother figures" from which the others are created; these tools range from the very simple to the impressively complex. These additional tools are conveniences, however, not necessities. I've cast charts and obtained clear answers to pressing questions using a ballpoint pen and a couple of sheets of notebook paper as my geomantic tools, and a concrete bench outside a grocery store as my working space.

In the more advanced, magical levels of geomancy, it's often useful to time divinations by a system of magical timekeeping known as *geomantic hours*. This system is covered in Chapter Seven, and can be left alone until then. All you need to know for now is that, just as nearly any place can be used by a geomancer as a working space, nearly any time is a good time to cast a geomantic chart.

The one exception is that it's normally not a good idea to cast a geomantic chart during a storm or other troubled weather. According to geomantic lore, the weather reflects the moods of the anima mundi, and unsettled conditions in the atmosphere are a good sign that the anima mundi may be too unsettled to bring you the knowledge you need. Ordinary wind and rain don't seem to be a problem, but if there's any sort of serious storm—especially if it involves lightning and thunder—it's traditional to wait until the weather clears before casting a chart.

In casting a geomantic chart, the state of the world around you is actually less important than the state of the "little world" that is yourself. Geomancy works best when it's approached with a calm mind and a willingness to let the figures turn out however they will. If your mind is troubled by anger or fear, these emotions will get in the way of the subtle interaction between your consciousness and the wider consciousness of the anima mundi. This can be a real challenge, especially if you're casting a chart about something that concerns you. The methods of preparing for divination covered in this lesson will help, but it's also useful to have at least one friend who also practices geomancy, and who can cast a chart for you whenever you're too emotionally involved in a situation to be able to cast one accurately for yourself.

Questions for Divination

Before you can begin the process of casting a chart, you need to decide on the question you want the chart to answer. Your questions provide the essential framework for the divination's meaning, the context in which the dance of geomantic figures can be understood.

What kinds of questions can be asked and answered by way of geomancy? In medieval and Renaissance Europe, when the art was at its height, nearly any question imaginable might be brought to a geomancer for a reading, including many that we would now answer through the use of very different resources. Weather prediction, for example, was a common subject for geomantic divination; the detection of thieves and the recovery of stolen property was another. People used geomancy to diagnose diseases, decide on routes for journeys, check the accuracy of news or rumors from distant places, choose strategies for warfare and other contests, find missing persons, test for pregnancy, and much more. Nowadays there are more reliable ways to find answers to some of these questions, but the world still has plenty of unknown factors at work, and geomancy can be used to sense how these will affect almost any area of human life.

Whatever the subject of the divination, the question needs to be thought out and phrased clearly before the process begins. There's little value in looking for an answer before you know the question! Take the time to think through the different aspects of the question, and to formulate what you want to know in a single sentence if at all possible. When the issues are unusually complex or emotionally difficult, it's often a good idea to write down all the factors you know about—those helping you deal with the situation as well as those hindering you—and search for common patterns. These often appear in readings as particular figures, and the more you know about them, the more easily you will recognize them and trace their interactions.

It's important to be sure the question says exactly what you want it to say. One of the most common mistakes in any form of divination is being careless about the question. When you cast a chart, you'll get the answer to the question that you asked, whether or not it's what you actually want to know! In other words, if you want to know whether a particular course of action is worth pursuing or not, don't ask something like "Is X a good idea?" X may be a great idea, but if you don't have the resources or talent to put it into practice, or something in the wider situation prevents it from going anywhere, even if it's the best idea in the world it can still be a complete waste of time and effort. Ask what you actually want to know by phrasing the question as "Would doing X accomplish Y?" or "Will the result of X be what I hope it will be?" The more clarity you put into your questions, the more clarity you'll get out of your readings.

If you do geomantic readings for anybody but yourself, you'll find that these problems are compounded many times over. I've learned that many people who come to me for advice have never actually thought through their questions, and the process of arriving at a clear question is sometimes enough, all by itself, to turn up the answer. It isn't always an answer they want to hear, however! People nowadays use divination and magic as a holding tank for many of their fantasies, unspoken desires, and fears. Keep that in mind when casting charts for others, and do your best to help them clarify exactly what it is they want to know.

Ethics of Divination

Ethical issues also deserve attention in divination, especially if you cast and interpret charts for anyone else. These issues partly unfold from the inherent uncertainty of any system of divination. The future can't be known until it actually happens, and the best that any system of divination can do is give the most likely outcome of a particular situation. Nor is even the best diviner infallible. When you set out to cast and interpret a chart, in other words, you've strayed past the bounds of honesty if you claim that you can predict the future perfectly, or provide absolutely certain answers to anything.

Your abilities as a geomancer, in addition, don't qualify you to practice medicine, psychotherapy, or any other professional discipline. It's entirely reasonable for you to cast and interpret charts for questions having to do with your own physical or mental health, so long as you remember that neither you nor geomancy is infallible, and you seek help from a qualified practitioner before you do anything that could endanger you or anyone else. It's not reasonable, nor is it legal, for you to cast and interpret charts to diagnose illnesses or prescribe treatments for anyone else. This is a serious matter; people have done jail time for claiming to be able to practice medicine using divinatory methods. Don't go there.

The problem, of course, is that people will ask you to do exactly that. If you become known, even among a small circle of friends, as a diviner, you can expect to have people you hardly know asking you for divinations about major life issues and serious crises—whether to let an unplanned pregnancy go to term, what to do about a life-threatening health problem, where to invest retirement funds, and the like. You'll need to know when to say no, and you may find it helpful to get contact information for the local crisis clinic, sources of low-cost emergency medical care, family planning resources, and the like.

The geomantic books of the Middle Ages and Renaissance are little help in these issues. Many of them give detailed instructions on how to cast and interpret charts for many questions that no ethical diviner will touch today. For example, "When will I die?" was a common question listed in the old books, and geomancers in the old days answered it without a second thought. If you decide to go beyond the material taught in this course and learn directly from the old geomantic literature, you'll need to be prepared for the difference between medieval and modern ethics, and work out your own code of ethics as a geomancer.

Equipment for Divination

Once the question has been settled, the next step in geomantic divination involves generating a set of four figures by some random method. Each of the sixteen figures is made up of four lines that are comprised of single or double points. A single point means that an element is manifest, a double point that the element is latent. By representing the single points with the number 1 and the double points with the number 0, the figures can be interpreted as numbers.

0010–1010–1101–0000

0011–0110–0100–1011

0101–1001–0001–1000

1110–0111–1100–1111

If you've had any exposure to what goes on inside the innards of today's computers, you'll recognize numbers like these at once. Binary or base-2 numbers are the foundation of modern computing, because an electrical circuit can have only two possible states: on or off. Our ordinary numbers are denary or base-10, meaning that any digit in a number can have any of ten different values: 0, 1, 2, 3, 4, 5, 6, 7, 8, or 9. In binary numbers, by contrast, the only options are 0 or 1; it's as simple as you can get and still have a number system at all.

In denary numbers, each digit is worth ten times as much as the digit to its right—consider the number 11, where the 1 on the left equals 10 and the 1 on the right is worth only 1. In binary numbers, each digit is worth twice as much as the digit to its right. So 1000, as a binary number, equals 8: (8 + 0 + 0 + 0). 0100 is 4, 0010 is 2, and 0001 is 1. Translated into denary numbers, the binary meanings of the sixteen figures in their traditional order work out to 2, 10, 13, 0, 3, 6, 4, 11, 5, 9, 1, 8, 14, 7, 12, and 15.

The binary meanings of the geomantic figures are mostly relevant to the most advanced levels of geomantic philosophy and practice, but the fact that geomantic figures are binary numbers has a very practical dimension. Anything, anything at all, that can give you one of two results— yes or no, even or odd, or what have you— four times is a workable way of generating geomantic figures. This is what allows for the diversity of geomancy tools, and it also allows you to cast a geomantic chart on the spur of the moment using anything that happens to come to hand.

In the earliest days of geomancy, the most common method that Arab geomancers used to cast a chart was to take a pointed stick, smooth out some desert sand, tap the stick on the sand a random number of times, and count the marks to see whether the result was odd or even. This process was repeated four times to make each figure. In the days when parchment was scarce and sand was plentiful, this method was very convenient, and traditional geomancers in the Arab countries and east Africa still use it today. If you live in a place where you have access to plenty of sand, it's an excellent method.

In the great cities of the medieval Arab world, however, the unmarked sands of the desert were a long walk away. Urban geomancers took early on to doing the same process with wax tablets—the common writing surface of the early Middle Ages—and with the coming of inexpensive paper in the Renaissance, paper and pen took over the same job. To use these or any other writing instruments, use the same method that the Arab wizards of old used on the desert sands: tap on the writing surface a random number of times, and count the result—even or odd—for each point of each figure you wish to cast. This was the approach that reached Europe first, and it remained the most common method straight through the Middle Ages and Renaissance. Still, it didn't take long before other methods came into use.

Dice, the most popular method of gambling in medieval Europe, also offered an effective way of casting geomantic readings. To use dice to create a figure, simply roll one die four times, and mark down whether the result of each roll is even or odd. The first roll is the head or Fire line, the second the neck or Air line, the third the body or Water line, and the fourth the feet or Earth line. Alternatively, get four dice of four different colors—if you can, red for Fire, yellow for Air, blue for Water, and green for Earth. Roll all four at once, and use each die to yield one line of a figure.

Some European and Middle Eastern museums have geomancy dice, which have single dots on three sides and double dots on the other three sides, but these are very hard to come by nowadays. A device that can still be found for sale in the Middle East consists of four geomantic dice on a spindle in a frame, arranged so that each one can be spun around independently with a flick of the finger. The diviner holds the frame and spins the four dice, producing an entire geomantic figure at once.

The great Renaissance geomancer Christopher Cattan commented that in his time, high-class prostitutes in Bologna used to cast geomantic charts with dried beans. They would pick up a small handful from a bowl, and then count to see whether they had an odd or even number in the handful; that gave them one line of a figure. The same thing can be done with a drawstring bag of small pebbles, which makes for a very portable and handy geomancy kit. One company, Rogue Regalia of Medford, Oregon (*www.rogueregalia.com*), makes and sells an elegant geomancy kit along these lines, comprised of a drawstring bag, a set of sixteen pebbles, and a casting cloth.

Cards have also been used for geomantic divination since shortly after they first arrived in Europe in the fourteenth century. To use a pack of ordinary playing cards to cast geomantic charts, remove the jokers, then shuffle, cut, and deal four cards. Red cards count as a single dot, black cards as a double dot. You could conceivably use a deck of Tarot cards for the same purpose—wands and swords count as one dot, cups and pentacles as two dots, and trumps are odd or even, depending on their number.

A few card decks designed specifically for geomancy have been produced in the last forty years or so, but the only one that is widely available at present is the Paracelsus Oracle Cards, produced by the Italian Tarot card manufacturers Lo Scarabeo. The Paracelsus deck has thirty-two cards, two for each of the sixteen figures. To use it for geomancy, get two sets and shuffle them together, so you have four of each figure. (It's rare for the same figure to turn up four times in a row in a standard geomantic reading, but this does happen.)

Much more cumbersome, though it's popular among ceremonial magicians in the Golden Dawn tradition, is an indoor equivalent of the desert sands used by the old Arab geomancers. Many Golden Dawn initiates build shallow wooden boxes, which are painted citrine, olive, russet, and black, and then filled with sand and consecrated with an elaborate ceremony. A two-foot length of a quarter-inch dowel with one end sharpened to a point (a pencil sharpener works well), also painted in these four colors, is similarly consecrated and used to make marks in the sand. If you decide to try this approach and own cats, you will need to make sure they don't mistake it for their catbox—and yes, this has happened! Instructions for making and consecrating this ornate style of geomantic gear can be found in books such as *Techniques of High Magic* by Francis King and Stephen Skinner and *Secrets of a Golden Dawn Temple* by Chic Cicero and Sandra Tabatha Cicero.

Going to the other end of the spectrum of complexity, a method for casting geomantic figures that was popular in pagan circles in the late twentieth century consists of four popsicle sticks. (For some unknown reason, these were called "Druid sticks"—geomancy has never been part of the Druid tradition, though some modern Druids do practice it.) Each stick has a single black dot in the middle of one side, and two black dots on the other. A mark on the end of each stick—the numbers 1 through 4, or the colors red for Fire, yellow for Air, blue for Water, and green for Earth—makes it easy to tell which line is which. It's not hard to produce something more attractive than a popsicle stick along the same lines if you have basic woodworking skills.

Finally, in our cybernetic age, it was inevitable that someone would come up with a geomancy computer program. Several online geomancy websites have web-based geomancy programs that will cast the figures for you and produce a chart. If you prefer a geomancy program with the same suite of features found in today's astrology programs, the astrologer and geomancer

Christopher Warnock has an excellent geomancy program, Geomanticon, available through his Renaissance Astrology website (*www.renaissanceastrology.com*); the program comes on a CD with a collection of four old geomantic texts in English, a bonus that could be useful to serious students of geomancy.

Preparing for Divination

Once you have settled on a question, made sure it asks what you actually want to know, thought through the ethical dimensions of the situation, and chosen your geomantic tools, the next step is to enter into a state of awareness that gives you access to the deeper, intuitive levels of your mind and allows you to access the wisdom of the anima mundi. This is both easier and more difficult than it may sound.

On the one hand, magical philosophy holds that no sharp divisions exist in the realm of consciousness. Each conscious being is a pattern in the flow of the anima mundi, a center where awareness gathers and deepens and then passes on. It's through this unifying flow of awareness that fads and a variety of other mass phenomena pass from mind to mind, and through the same flow that human beings naturally connect to the broader consciousness of the Earth and the universe as a whole.

On the other hand, many of the common habits of human thought, and in particular many of the ways people in the modern world are taught to use their minds, get in the way of this natural linkage to the flow of consciousness. The task of the geomancer is to get these blockages out of the way, by stilling the ordinary thinking mind. This is simple enough— but "simple," of course, is not always the same thing as "easy."

The necessary shift in awareness can be made in any number of ways, ranging from the simple act of clearing the mind to complex ritual processes drawn from the lore of ceremonial magic. We'll explore two particular methods here, one simple, one a little more complex—either one will do the trick. Some people will find that one method works best for them, while others may find both equally effective. It's also entirely appropriate to come up with a method of your own. Here as so often in geomancy, the personal equation is the deciding factor.

Contemplative Method

The first method is done entirely within the mind. If you practice meditation or have a talent for it, you're likely to find this method easy. Otherwise, it may take some work to master.

Simply close your eyes and draw your attention inward. Make your mind as clear as possible; let thoughts, worries, and outside factors fall away. After you reach a space of clarity, center your mind on the question you want to answer through divination. Don't "think about" the question in the usual sense of that phrase; instead, hold the question in your mind, keeping your attention on it and leaving the whole array of potential consequences, worries, hopes, and fears outside. Let your awareness settle into place, and allow all other issues to fade from the center of attention. When you are able to focus yourself in this way, begin the divination process.

The skill of stilling your mind and then bringing your attention to bear on a single subject is central to certain advanced methods of geomantic practice. For this reason, among others, the contemplative method is worth exploring, even if it seems challenging at first. It also forms the first step on the path toward geomantic meditation, an important branch of geomantic practice that will be covered in detail in Chapter Eight.

Theurgic Method

The second method of preparing for geomantic divination uses the symbols and practices of Renaissance theurgy—the magical art of entering into contact with spiritual beings. While this is only one of many possible ways to enter into contact with the spiritus mundi, it has deep roots in geomantic tradition, for geomancy is a way of magic as well as a method of divination.

What is magic? Modern occultists have one set of answers to this crucial question, scientists have another, and of course the mainstream religions of the Western world have answers of their own, based more on superstition and prejudice than anything else. It's important to understand, though, that medieval and Renaissance mages answered this question in their own way. To them, as we saw back in Chapter One, everything was composed of corpus (body) or physical form, spiritus (life-spirit) or vital energy, and anima (soul) or conscious essence, and patterns in the anima mundi cascaded down via the spiritus mundi into material form in the corpus mundi.

Magic, from this perspective, is the art of finding the appropriate patterns in the anima mundi and opening a channel for those patterns in the spiritus mundi, so they manifest in the corpus mundi in a particular way. Speaking of patterns in the anima mundi makes them seem abstract and impersonal, however, and to the mages of the Renaissance they were nothing of the kind. Everything that exists in the realm of the anima mundi is a soul, and so these "patterns" are also beings. Each has its own spiritus and corpus, just as we do. When the old magical books speak of spirits, they're talking about beings who differ from humanity in having bodies of a subtler form of matter than we do. The art of theurgy—literally "divine work," from the Greek words *theos*, "god," and *ourgia*, "work"—is the branch of traditional magic that works directly with such beings.

Fourteen of these spirits have a close connection to geomancy. Seven of them are called planetary intelligences, and represent patterns of consciousness in the anima mundi that relate to the seven planets of traditional astrology. The other seven are called planetary spirits; they are reflections of the planetary intelligences in the spiritus mundi.

Geomantic lore has it that one of these seven spirits, guided by its governing intelligence, directs the hand of the geomancer in any geomantic divination. Strange as this may sound from a modern point of view, it indicates an important facet of the divination process. Like every other form of divination, geomancy depends on reading meaning from events not controlled by the diviner's conscious mind. Where, then, do the messages in geomantic readings come from? Most people nowadays might say chance, or synchronicity, or perhaps the subconscious mind. Yet if you can ask chance, synchronicity, or the subconscious mind a question and get a useful answer, then for all practical purposes chance, synchronicity, and the unconscious mind fill exactly the same role as spirits such as Hismael and Sorath. In either case, the diviner asks a question and receives an intelligent answer from a disembodied source. It would not be going too far to think of chance, synchronicity, and the unconscious mind as names for three of the familiar spirits of modern industrial society.

Some geomancers nowadays prefer to invoke these spirits in place of the planetary spirits and intelligences of occult tradition. Still, the older lore offers major advantages; it provides an effective, integrated tool kit of divinatory and magical methods, far more thoroughly developed than the rudimentary methods worked out by modern psychologists. This is hardly the fault of modern psychologists; they have only had one hundred fifty years to work out their methods, while magicians have been developing theirs for millennia.

The seven planetary spirits of geomantic lore have a name, a symbol or sigil, and a range of human experiences and activities with which they resonate. These are:

 Zazel corresponds to the planet Saturn, and governs time, death, agriculture and building, abstract thought, and philosophy, as well as all things relating to the past. His intelligence is Agiel.

 Hismael corresponds to the planet Jupiter, and governs good fortune, growth and expansion, formal ceremonies and rites of passage, charity, feasting, and advancement in one's profession or in any organization. His intelligence is Yophiel.

Table 4-1 The Geomantic Intelligences and Spirits

Planet	Intelligence	Spirit	Figures
Saturn	Agiel	Zazel	Carcer, Tristitia (Cauda Draconis)
Jupiter	Yophiel	Hismael	Acquisitio, Laetitia (Caput Draconis)
Mars	Graphiel	Bartzabel	Puer, Rubeus
Sun	Nakhiel	Sorath	Fortuna Major, Fortuna Minor
Venus	Hagiel	Kedemel	Amissio, Puella
Mercury	Tiriel	Taphthartharath	Albus, Conjunctio
Moon	(see note)	Chashmodai	Populus, Via

Note: Instead of a single governing intelligence, the Moon has an Intelligence of Intelligences named Malkah be-Tarshishim ve-ad Ruachoth Shechalim, and a Spirit of Spirits named Shad Barshemoth ha-Shartathan.

Bartzabel corresponds to the planet Mars, and governs competition, war, destruction, surgery, male sexuality, and matters connected with livestock. His intelligence is Graphiel.

Sorath corresponds to the Sun, and governs power, leadership, positions of authority, success, balance and reconciliation, and sports and games involving physical effort. His intelligence is Nakhiel.

Kedemel corresponds to the planet Venus, and governs art, music and dance, social occasions and enjoyments, pleasures, love, the emotions generally, and female sexuality. Her intelligence is Hagiel.

Taphthartharath corresponds to the planet Mercury, and governs learning, messages, communication, all intellectual pursuits, gambling, medicine and healing, trade, economic matters, trickery, deception, and theft. Its intelligence is Tiriel.

Chashmodai corresponds to the Moon, and governs journeys, the sea, hunting and fishing, biological cycles, reproduction and childbirth, psychic phenomena, dreams, the unconscious, and the unknown. Unlike the other planetary spirits, she has two higher patterns of consciousness above her: an Intelligence of Intelligences, Malkah be-Tarshishim ve-ad Ruachoth Shechalim, and a Spirit of Spirits, Shad Barshemoth ha-Shartathan.

The first step in this approach to preparing for divination, then, is to select the one of these seven powers that relates most closely to the question you intend to ask. Once you have done this, draw a circle a few inches across on the sand or Earth you will be using for the divination, if you are using this most traditional method, or on the paper you will be using to record the divination. Then draw the sigil of the planetary spirit governing the question at the center of the circle. The final result, shown with the sigil of Sorath as an example, should look like Figure 4-1.

Figure 4-1 Invoking the Spirit

Now concentrate on the symbol you have drawn, and as in the first method of preparation, center your mind on the question you wish the divination to answer. Once you have achieved the state of balanced focus, begin the divination process.

After the divination has been completed, the link established between your consciousness and the planetary spirit should be released; otherwise, that particular aspect of the anima mundi is likely to remain stronger than usual in your life for some time, producing a range of potential imbalances. To close off the link, simply retrace the circle counterclockwise, banishing the forces you have summoned.

Casting the Four Mothers

Once you have settled on a question, chosen your tools, and prepared yourself for the divination, you can proceed to cast a full geomantic reading. Instead of producing a single figure, the way Chapter One showed you how to do, you'll need to cast four figures, which are called the Four Mothers. These produce four more, the Four Daughters, and the Mothers and Daughters between them give rise to other figures—Nieces, Witnesses, and a Judge—to fill up the complete chart. This takes a little more time than just casting a single figure, but it allows the figures to offer a precise and detailed answer to the question you ask.

Start your divination by casting four figures, using whatever method you prefer. These are called the Four Mothers because they give birth to all the other figures. Once you have the Four Mothers, you can put your casting tools away. All the other figures are created out of the Four Mothers by various methods, and go in their own places on the shield chart, the first and most basic style of geomantic chart. The shield chart, with the place of the Mothers marked on it, is shown in Figure 4-2.

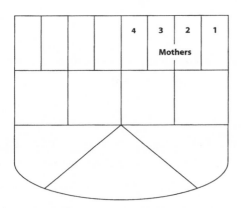

Figure 4-2 The Four Mothers

The Art and Practice of Geomancy

The Four Daughters

The Mothers then give birth to the next four figures, the four Daughters, by a simple process of rearrangement. The First Daughter is born by taking the head of each of the Four Mothers in order: thus, the head of the First Mother becomes the First Daughter's head, the head of the Second Mother becomes the First Daughter's neck, the head of the Third Mother becomes the First Daughter's body, and the head of the Fourth Mother becomes the First Daughter's feet. In the same way, the necks of the Mothers make the Second Daughter, their bodies the Third Daughter, and their feet the Fourth Daughter, as shown in Figure 4-3. The daughters then go in their own places in the shield chart, as shown in Figure 4-4.

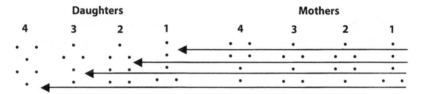

Figure 4-3 Making the Daughters

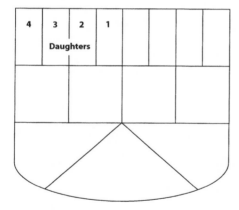

Figure 4-4 The Four Daughters

The Four Nieces

At this point a third process comes into play, creating what the medieval handbooks call the Four Nieces (the Four Nephews in modern books on geomancy). Start with the First and Second Mothers, which combine to create the First Niece. Add together the points in each line of these two Mothers. If the two Mothers have the same head—both of them have a single point, or both have a double—the heads of the Mothers add up to 2 or 4, both even numbers, and the head of the Niece is a double point. If the Mothers have different heads—one has a single point and the other a double point—they add up to 3, an odd number, and the Niece's head is a single point. Add the necks, bodies, and feet of the Mothers in the same way, and the resulting figure is the First Niece. Figure 4-5 shows how this works.

•	•	+	•	•	=	•	•	2 dots + 2 dots = even number = 2 dots
	•	+	•	•	=	•		1 dot + 2 dots = odd number = 1 dot
•	•	+	•		=	•		2 dots + 1 dot = odd number = 1 dot
	•	+	•		=	•	•	1 dot + 1 dot = even number = 2 dots

Figure 4-5 Making the Nieces

In the same way, the Third and Fourth Mothers produce the Second Niece, the First and Second Daughters the Third Niece, and the Third and Fourth Daughters the Fourth Niece, as shown in Figure 4-6.

The Witnesses and Judge

The same process that produces the Nieces goes further, giving birth to three more figures: the Witnesses and the Judge. The Right Witness is created by adding together the First and Second Nieces, and the Left Witness by adding together the Third and Fourth Nieces. The Witnesses go into the chart as shown in Figure 4-7.

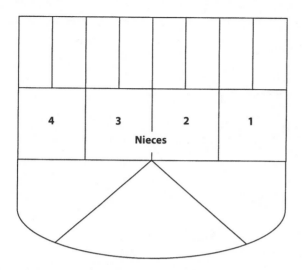

Figure 4-6 The Four Nieces

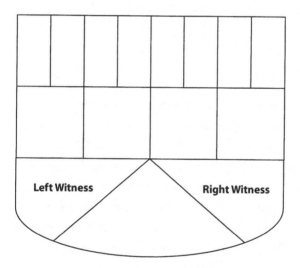

Figure 4-7 The Left and Right Witnesses

Finally, the Judge is created by adding together the Witnesses according to the same process, and goes into the chart in its own place.

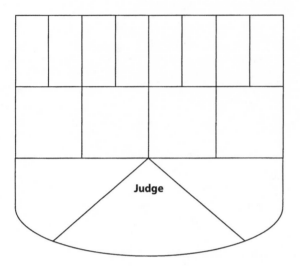

Figure 4-8 The Judge

The mathematical process that creates each geomantic reading has a curious effect that allows the diviner to check his or her accuracy. Since the same points differently arranged make up the Mothers and the Daughters, the Judge—the only figure generated from both sides of the reading—will always be made up by an even number of points. As a result, only eight of the sixteen figures—Amissio, Populus, Fortuna Major, Conjunctio, Carcer, Acquisitio, Fortuna Minor, and Via—can be the Judge in a reading. If you get any other figure for the Judge, you need to go back and double-check your addition.

CHAPTER FIVE

INTERPRETING THE SHIELD CHART

At the end of the process described in Chapter Four, you've generated the complete set of geomantic figures you'll need for a reading, and the mechanical part of geomantic divination is over. What remains is the interpretation of the chart, where the patterns that have come out of this first phase become bearers of meaning.

The process of interpreting a divination has had far too much mystery built up around it. In an important sense, interpretation is simply telling a story. The *querent*—the person for whom the chart has been cast, whether this is the geomancer or someone else—is the main character, and the *quesited*—the person or thing the querent wants to know about—is the driving force behind the plot. The geomantic figures are the sixteen basic plot elements the storyteller has to work with. The setting and the characters of the story unfold out of the question the divination is meant to answer.

It can be a useful exercise to look at each of the sixteen figures in this way, and think of them as chapters in a story. In the Amissio chapter, for example, the main character loses something important; in the Carcer chapter, the walls of a prison close around him; in the Via chapter, a long journey leads away into the distance, and so on. Read in this way, the traditional sequence of the sixteen figures—like the sequence of trumps in the Tarot deck—tells a specific and very important story, a story of spiritual maturation and unfoldment. That story provides the central framework for a geomantic way of initiation, which you can encounter and explore through the tools of geomantic meditation and scrying covered in Chapter Eight of this book. For now, as you work with the figures in your divinations, see whether you can sense the flow and pattern of that story of initiation and explore how it applies to your own life.

From a certain perspective, the story of initiation is the most important story that can be told, but it's only one of countless stories woven from the sixteen geomantic figures. In your work with geomantic divination, you'll be spending most of your time with these other stories, exploring the events of your own life and the experiences and questions of those who come to you for advice. Since geomancy has only sixteen figures, you'll need to use your own intuition, prompted by the symbolism of the figures and the meanings of the different positions in the two geomantic charts, to fill in the details of those stories and bring each reading into clear focus. This is why it's a waste of time to do as most of the few modern books on geomancy advise, and interpret a geomantic chart by looking up canned answers from a table. "Evil, except for bloodletting" and "For love, good; for sickness, evil" are complete entries from the most widely copied set of geomantic tables used nowadays, the one given in the Golden Dawn knowledge lecture mentioned in Chapter One; they give so little information that it's no wonder geomancy has been so neglected in recent years. The intuition of the geomancer, guided by experience, a solid understanding of the symbolism and meanings of the sixteen figures, and a mastery of the divinatory process, is far more useful than any set of tables because it allows the patterns of meaning in each divination to come through clearly. It's because of this that each geomancer comes to understand the figures in a uniquely personal way.

The Querent and the Quesited

There are many different ways to read a geomantic chart, depending on the level of detail you need and the level of skill you've reached. The shield chart, which was introduced in Chapter Four, is the framework for the most basic methods of interpretation. In geomancy, as in anything else, it's a good idea to start with the simplest methods, master those first, and then move on to the more complex ones. This is why we're starting with the last three figures of the shield chart, and moving step by step through more complex methods; this will allow you to study and learn them in a sequence that makes sense.

The foundation level of any geomantic reading is the meaning of the two Witnesses and the Judge. You can get a fairly good answer in many readings by interpreting the Judge alone, as though you'd cast it in a one-figure reading. If your question can be answered with a yes or no, a favorable Judge means yes, an unfavorable one no. You can often answer more complex questions by paying attention to the meanings and symbolism of the Judge. Add the Witnesses and you have a basic reading that gives a great deal of information at a glance. The Right Witness represents the querent, and everything the querent brings into the situation. Similarly, the Left Witness represents the quesited, and everything the quesited brings into the situation. The Judge stands for the relationship between querent and quesited. The Right Witness is also the past, since the querent's past experiences are among the most important things he or she brings to the question. The Judge is also the present, since the querent's relationship to the quesited is brought into focus at the time of the divination. The Left Witness is also the future, since the most important factors the quesited brings to the situation are the potentials it holds for the querent's future life.

The Witnesses also influence the overall meaning of the reading. Thus a favorable Judge derived from two favorable Witnesses becomes even more favorable, while an unfavorable Judge derived from two unfavorable Witnesses becomes even more unfavorable. If the Witnesses and Judge are a mix of favorable and unfavorable figures, this suggests that in the subject of the divination, as so often in life, positive and negative factors are mixed, and it also gives specific hints about the way these shape the situation. Put the three figures together into a story, as suggested above, and you'll see how this works.

Let's look at some common patterns. Whenever the Right Witness is a figure favorable to the question it implies that the querent is in a strong position at the beginning of the situation, while an unfavorable Right Witness shows that the querent's position is weak. Beyond its favorable or unfavorable qualities, the figure that appears as Right Witness also comments about the querent's own attitude and agenda. When Puer is the Right Witness, for example, the querent is usually approaching the situation with more enthusiasm than common sense; when Populus is the Right Witness, the querent often hasn't thought through the situation at all, and is simply doing what other people expect him or her to do; when Via is the Right Witness, the querent's interest in the quesited may be a temporary thing that will soon pass off, and so on.

A favorable Left Witness shows that the quesited is something that would benefit the querent, while an unfavorable Left Witness shows that the quesited is something that will harm the querent. If the quesited is something the querent wants, and the Left Witness is an unfavorable figure, this often means it's something the querent would be better off without. The figure that appears as Left Witness gives information about the quesited, but this information focuses on what the quesited means to the querent. When Rubeus is the Left Witness, for example, it's fair to say that the quesited arouses strong and dangerous passions in the querent; whether the quesited is passionate and dangerous, though, is another matter, and has to be read elsewhere in the chart.

The Judge, as explained above, describes the interaction between the querent and quesited. As explained in Chapter Four, the Judge will always be one of the following eight figures: Amissio, Populus, Fortuna Major, Conjunctio, Carcer, Acquisitio, Fortuna Minor, and Via. Each pair of Witnesses can produce only one Judge. This points to one of the major differences between geomancy and some other divination methods, such as Tarot. When you cast a Tarot reading, any card can show up next to any other card; the only thing that normally won't happen is to have the same card next to itself—the Six of Swords, say, next to another Six of Swords.

In geomancy, by contrast, if you have Puer as the Right Witness and Rubeus as the Left Witness, you'll inevitably get Carcer as the Judge; if you have Puella as the Right Witness and Laetitia as the Left Witness, you'll always have Acquisitio as the Judge; if you have Fortuna Minor as both Right and Left Witness—and this sort of thing happens in geomancy—you can count on Populus as the Judge, and so on. It's rather like mathematics: given querent X and quesited Y, you can count on relationship Z. In fact, because of the internal mathematics of geomancy, there are only 128 possible combinations of Right Witness, Left Witness, and Judge.

This is one of the limitations of this most basic way of interpreting a geomantic chart, but like most limitations, it's also a strength. As you study geomancy and learn to apply its lessons to the events of daily life, you'll find yourself recognizing the same patterns of querent and quesited in the events around you, and you'll find as a result that you can predict in advance the way their relationship will work out, even if you don't take the time to cast a geomantic chart.

Sample Readings

A few examples will help make these methods clearer. Figure 5-1 (page 92) shows the first of these. The querent works at a company that has been forced to lay off several hundred staff members. His position will be terminated shortly. His supervisor, though, has offered him another position with the same company. He wants to know if he should accept the new position or simply wrap up his involvement with the company and look elsewhere.

The chart in Figure 5-1, which has Cauda Draconis for the Right Witness and Laetitia for the Left Witness, has Conjunctio as Judge. Cauda Draconis is an unfavorable, disruptive figure, good only for losses and

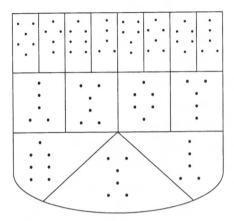

Figure 5-1 Sample Reading 1

endings; it very likely refers to the end of the querent's current position. Laetitia is favorable in almost any question. The Judge, Conjunctio, is a neutral figure, meaning a combination of forces for good or ill; under the influence of one positive and one negative Witness, it keeps this neutral quality.

Factoring in the element of time, this combination shows a pattern of events in which the querent has suffered a significant loss, but as a result of a combination of factors in the present, the future is very bright indeed. The chart suggests that the new position he has been offered is worth accepting, and may have unexpected benefits—for example, a promotion to a better position somewhere down the line.

The second reading is shown in Figure 5-2. The querent, a single woman, has been involved in a relationship with a married lover. While she enjoys the freedom and the romantic dimension of the relationship, her lover's repeated claims that he will shortly leave his wife and marry her have begun to ring hollow, since the relationship has gone on for more than a year and the lover has shown no signs of following up on his promises. She wants to know where the relationship is headed.

Here Puella is the Right Witness and Albus is the Left, with Carcer for the Judge. Carcer is a profoundly unfavorable figure in matters of the heart; the effect of two favorable Witnesses makes it less negative, but its basic meaning of limitation and restriction does not change, and it suggests that the relationship will never be anything more than it is at the time of the reading. Puella represents the emotions and romantic ideas that led the querent into this relationship, while Albus, a figure of wisdom and self-knowledge, suggests that the querent needs to take a hard look at her own motives and needs before she invests more time and emotion in the current situation.

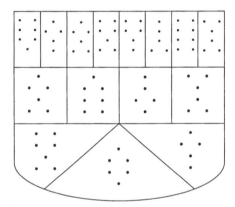

Figure 5-2 Sample Reading 2

The third reading is shown in Figure 5-3. The querent is a writer who has just finished her first novel and is looking for a publisher. At a literary event in the city she lives in, she met an agent who expressed interest in seeing her manuscript. She is not certain, however, if the contract with the agent is worth pursuing or not.

In this reading the Right Witness is Conjunctio, the Left Witness is Acquisitio, and the Judge is Fortuna Major. Conjunctio is a neutral figure, meaning a combination of forces, while Fortuna Major and Acquisitio are the best figures of the sixteen. Conjunctio, representing the past and her own contribution to the situation, very likely stands for her contact with the agent; Fortuna Major, as the present, suggests that the connection she has established is very much worth following up, while Acquisitio, as the future, predicts that the agent will be able to find a publisher for her novel.

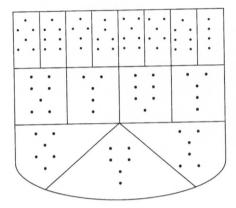

Figure 5-3 Sample Reading 3

The Way of the Points

Another basic tool for interpreting a geomantic chart allows the diviner to find out the root of the question—the factor, often unknown to the querent, that provides the driving force behind the whole situation. This is determined by a method called the Way of the Points.

The Way of the Points unfolds on the complete shield chart, starting with the Judge. Look at the first element, the head or Fire line of the Judge, and note whether it is a single or a double point. Then go to the Witnesses, and see if either of them has the same first line. If not—if, as in Figure 5-1, the Judge has a double point as its head, but each of the Witnesses has a single point—the Way of the Points cannot be formed, and this suggests that the situation is exactly what it seems. If one of the Witnesses has the same head as the Judge, however, the Way of the Points moves from the Judge to that Witness.

From here you repeat the same process, checking the two Nieces that give birth to the Witness in question to see if either has the same first line. If so, the Way of the Points goes to that Niece; if not, it stops at the Witness. From the Niece the Way of the Points goes to the Daughters or Mothers, depending on which Niece is involved, and once again you check the two figures who give birth to the Niece to see if either or both of them share the same first line.

Wherever the Way of the Points comes to an end, whether it's the Judge, a Witness, a Niece, or a Daughter or Mother, is the root factor or factors of the situation, and should be taken as a guide to the inner nature of the question and the true driving forces behind it.

The mathematics of geomancy have an interesting effect on the Way of the Points. If the Fire line of the Judge is a single point, the Way of the Points will always be formed, and will always follow an unbranching path up to one of the Mothers or Daughters. If the Judge's Fire line is a double point, on the other hand, the Way of the Points—if it forms at all—will always branch, and always end at more than one figure. In exceptional cases, it can include every figure in the chart!

This represents a source of insight. Of the eight figures that can be the Judge, four—Amissio, Carcer, Fortuna Minor, and Via—begin with a single point, and four—Populus, Fortuna Major, Conjunctio, and Acquisitio—begin with a double point. Situations of the sort described by the first four often have a single root cause, whether or not this is visible at first glance. Situations of the sort described by the second four, on the other hand, often have more diffuse causes.

If we turn back to the three sample readings above, the Way of the Points can be used to learn more about the deeper factors at work in each one. In the first example, Figure 5-1, the Way of the Points cannot be formed; the Judge, Conjunctio, has two points in its Fire line, while both of the Witnesses have one. This means that there is no particular meaning or driving force behind the loss of the querent's job. It happened, it's over with, and now it's time to move on and deal with the potentialities of the future.

In the second example, Figure 5-2, the Way of the Points can be formed. Carcer, the Judge, has one point as its Fire line; so does the Right Witness, Puella; so does the Second Niece, Puer, and so does the Third Mother, Cauda Draconis. This last figure is perhaps the most difficult of the sixteen, and represents losses, endings, and disruptions. It's possible, therefore, that the querent's commitment to her relationship comes out of some source of unhappiness elsewhere in her life. She should explore this possibility, get help if she needs it, and try to resolve the underlying issue before she makes a final decision about the relationship.

In the third example, Figure 5-3, the Way of the Points can be formed but branches widely, including both Witnesses, all four Nieces, and the Third and Fourth Mothers. These last two figures are the most important factors, but the First, Third, and Fourth Nieces are also ends of the Way of the Points and may be considered in the interpretation. The Mothers suggest that an important factor in the querent's success is a willingness to balance her passion for her writing (Rubeus, the Fourth Mother) with the practical concerns of the business side of writing (Acquisitio, the Third Mother). Caput Draconis, which appears twice as the First and Third Niece, suggests that her position as a writer just starting her career may be an advantage to her.

The Four Triplicities

Another basic approach to geomantic interpretation makes use of four triplicities, or sets of three figures, drawn from the first twelve figures in the chart. These are often used in general readings done to tell a querent about the overall patterns at work in his or her life; they can also be combined with the Witnesses and Judge to relate a more specific question to the broader picture of the querent's life. They form an intermediate step between the methods we've already covered and the twelve houses, where the higher reaches of geomantic divination begin.

Each of the four Nieces, together with the two Mothers or Daughters that produce it, makes up one of the triplicities, as shown in Figure 5-4. The triplicities, their figures, and their meanings are as follows:

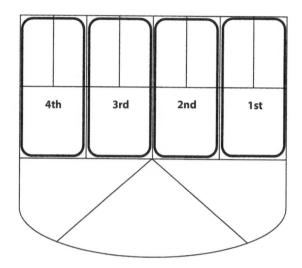

Figure 5-4 The Four Triplicities

The first triplicity consists of the First and Second Mother and the First Niece. It stands for the querent, including his or her circumstances, health, habits, and outlook on life.

The second triplicity consists of the Third and Fourth Mothers and the Second Niece. It stands for the events shaping the querent's life at the time of the reading.

The third triplicity consists of the First and Second Daughters and the Third Niece. It stands for the querent's home and work environment, the places he or she frequents, and the kind of people he or she meets there. Family members and housemates appear in this triplicity.

The fourth triplicity consists of the Third and Fourth Daughters and the Fourth Niece. It stands for the querent's friends, associates, and authority figures.

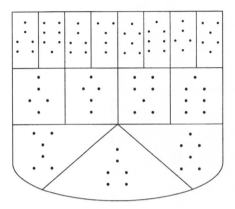

Figure 5-5 Sample Reading 4

Read each triplicity as though the Niece were a Judge and the two Mothers or Daughters were the Right and Left Witnesses. The sample reading in Figure 5-5 shows how this works.

Here the querent is troubled about the way his life is going and wants to understand what's happening. The first triplicity—Acquisitio, Puer, and Laetitia—describes the querent himself: passionate, forceful, energetic, and generally successful in life. He has made gains in the past (Acquisitio) and pursues the things he wants with energy and enthusiasm (Puer), and for the moment the results are good (Laetitia). He's likely to rush into things without looking first, but tends to get out of the resulting scrapes by a combination of Puer's energy and sheer luck, a common meaning of Laetitia.

The second triplicity—Laetitia, Amissio, and Albus—shows the current influences at work in his life. Here he is facing the possibility of a significant loss in the future (Amissio). He may not be able to rely on things that have worked in the past (Laetitia) to get him through this, since his present situation (Albus) is favorable but weak. The one potential bright spot is that Amissio, while unfavorable in most things, is favorable for love. As the next triplicity shows, this may be an important factor.

The third triplicity—Caput Draconis, Fortuna Minor, and Puella—describes the places where he spends his time and the people with whom he associates there. Here the central factor is Puella, who quite possibly shows a love interest; Puella often means this in readings for heterosexual men or lesbians. (Puer has the same meaning in readings for heterosexual women or gay men.) Caput Draconis shows that this is a fairly new thing; either he's recently met the person in question or he's recently passed through personal changes that make this relationship possible. Fortuna Minor suggests that he's not finished changing, though, and the approaching changes are likely to be quick and unexpected.

The fourth triplicity—Tristitia, Fortuna Minor, and Puer—reveals the querent's friends and associates. Tristitia suggests a quality of "stuckness" to the querent's relationships; perhaps he and his associates or coworkers are caught in quarrels and unsatisfactory interactions that repeat like a broken record. Puer suggests that conflict is a real possibility, though emotional stress rather than any deeper factor is likely to be the cause. Fortuna Minor hints that this is another situation ripe for change, and suggests that the querent may find it best to seek help in resolving things constructively.

The triplicities provide the pattern that's summed up by the Witnesses and Judge. The Right Witness is Amissio, the Left Witness Conjunctio, and the Judge Fortuna Minor, suggesting that the same process of rapid change that appears elsewhere in the reading is the keynote of his life at the present time. The querent's own situation is defined by loss and the possibility of love, and he is moving toward an intersection of new possibilities, quite possibly associated with his new relationship, a common meaning of Conjunctio. Right now change catalyzed by factors outside himself is the central theme in his life. He needs to give these changes the time they need, to be willing to give up old habits and assumptions, and to welcome new potentials as they open up for him. The troubles he is facing at this point in his life are transitory, and in the long run he can expect better things.

CHAPTER SIX

INTERPRETING THE HOUSE CHART

The methods of basic interpretation covered in Chapter Five—the inter-pretation of Witnesses and Judge, the Way of the Points, and the four tri-plicities—yield an overall response to any question, but it's often useful to get a more detailed view of the situation, and see how specific issues are affected by the pattern of forces at work in the reading. In this case the focus of interpretation shifts, and the figures are read, not according to their "he-redity" on the shield chart, but by their placement in the twelve geomantic houses. These twelve houses, like the twelve houses of astrology on which they're modeled, serve to map out parts of human life affected by forces at work in the querent's life. (See Figure 6-1 on page 102).

The first twelve figures of the chart—the Mothers, Daughters, and Nieces—go into the twelve houses of the house chart. Some systems of geomancy have complicated ways of doing this, but the traditional method is simplicity itself: the twelve figures are put into the twelve houses in their order of creation. The First Mother, in other words, becomes the figure in the first house, the Second Mother goes in the second house, and so on until the Fourth and final Niece is placed in the twelfth house.

A detail of geomantic tradition probably needs to be discussed at this point. In some books on geomancy, you'll encounter the claim that the

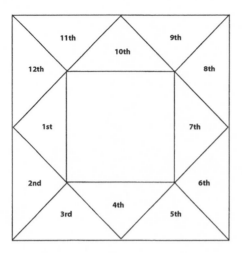

Figure 6-1 The Twelve Houses

figures Rubeus and Cauda Draconis are unspeakably bad omens if they appear in the first house of a geomantic chart. When this happens, the geomancer is supposed to stop the divination, destroy the chart, and wait at least two hours before trying again.

This started out as a useful piece of advice drawn from the old geomantic texts. According to these teachings, Rubeus in the first house means that the querent is not being honest with the geomancer, and Cauda Draconis in the first house means that the querent has already decided what to do and won't listen to a reading that disagrees with his or her preconceptions. If you get either of these figures in a reading for somebody else, then you may be wise to be on your guard. Equally, another rule from the same traditional sources—watching out for Populus in the first house and Rubeus in the eleventh, which means the querent has made up a fake question to try to trick the geomancer—is worth following. All these will be discussed in more detail in Chapter Seven.

Still, it's not necessary to stop a reading if any of these signs appear. If you feel comfortable doing so, you might mention the traditional meaning of the figure and ask the querent if it might have any bearing on the reading. If you are doing a reading for yourself, on the other hand, confront yourself directly: Are you being honest with yourself? Will you listen if the reading tells you your preconceptions are wrong? Is the question you're asking what you really want to know about? All these can be potent opportunities for self-knowledge.

The Twelve Houses

In any geomantic reading on the house chart, the first house is called the *house of the querent*, and the figure there is the *significator of the querent*. One of the other houses—the house corresponding to the question being asked—is called the *house of the quesited*, and the figure there is the *significator of the quesited*. The meanings of the houses are given below.

The First House

The first house, as just mentioned, traditionally represents the querent, the person about whom the divination is performed. Divinations for newborn children often assign the child to the first house, and then read off each aspect of the child's future life around the circle of the houses. Readings for days, weeks, months, and years assign the first house to the querent's personality and read off the different departments of his or her life from the other houses. These and several similar methods, however, belong to the special questions covered in Chapter Seven. For the standard house chart reading, the first house represents the querent, while the quesited belongs to one of the other houses of the chart.

The Second House

The second house traditionally governs money and movable property. Any question having to do with profit and loss, income, investments, personal belongings, thefts, and the like takes the figure in the second house as the significator of the quesited. The exceptions to this rule are real estate, which belongs to the fourth house, and speculative investments, which belong to the fifth. Questions belonging to the second house include:

- Will my business make or lose money?
- Will the investment be profitable?
- Will I get paid for the work I did?
- Is this a good time to borrow money?
- Is the antique table worth what the seller is asking?
- Will the package I shipped arrive safely?
- Has my missing watch been stolen?
- Will my stolen car be recovered?

The Third House

The third house traditionally governs the querent's brothers and sisters, neighbors, and immediate surroundings. It also rules journeys of less than 200 miles, education from preschool through high school, advice, news, and rumors. Questions assigned to the third house include:

- Will my relationship with my sister improve?
- Will the neighbors agree to an easement?
- Is this a good weekend to drive to the beach?

- Should I enroll my child in North Central Elementary?
- Is my neighbor George's advice worth following?
- Is the news story accurate?
- Should I believe the rumors?

The Fourth House

The fourth house traditionally governs land, agriculture, building, cities and towns, relocation and moving, anything underground, any unknown object, ancient places and things, old age, the querent's father, and the end of any matter. Questions appropriate to the fourth house include:

- Is the property worth buying?
- Is the soil fertile?
- Will roses flourish here?
- Should I move to another apartment?
- Is Springfield a good place to relocate?
- Is the table antique or a modern reproduction?
- Is the pension fund in reliable hands?
- How is my father doing?
- How will the present situation turn out in the end?

The Fifth House

The fifth house traditionally governs crops from perennial or biennial plants, fertility, pregnancy, and children. Sexuality belongs here, but not love or marriage, which are assigned to the seventh house. Parties and entertainment of all kinds, food and drink, and clothing also belong to the fifth house, along with bodies of water, fishing, and rain.

Finally, letters and messages belong here, and so do books; back in the Middle Ages, a common question for geomancy was whether some book contained accurate information or not—a question that might be worth asking more often nowadays! Questions assigned to the fifth house include:

- Will the grape crop be good this year?
- Is Janis interested in me sexually?
- Is my unborn child a boy or a girl?
- How well will my four-year-old cope with a baby brother?
- Will the concert be worth the ticket price?
- Is next Friday a good night for the party?
- Is the new Asian restaurant in town worth a visit?
- Will the dress be ready in time for the wedding?
- How will fishing be on the lake this weekend?
- Will it rain tomorrow?
- Will I receive a letter from my grandmother?
- Are the claims in the book I'm reading accurate?

The Sixth House

The sixth house traditionally governs the querent's employees, and people in all service professions from physicians to plumbers, entertainers, and prostitutes. It governs practitioners of magic and occultism other than the querent. It also governs pets, and all domestic animals except horses, donkeys, mules, cattle, and camels. Finally, it governs illnesses and injuries. Questions appropriate to the sixth house include:

- Should I hire Phyllis?
- Are my employees stealing from the till?
- Are the plumbers reliable?
- Should I hire a band for the party?
- Will I find my lost dog?
- Will hogs fetch a good price this fall?
- How serious is this illness?
- Would it be worthwhile to get a Tarot reading from Marie?
- Is this a good time to have dental work done?
- Will I catch flu this winter?

The Seventh House

The seventh house traditionally governs the most intense human relationships. The querent's spouse or lover belongs here, along with everything related to love and marriage. Partnerships, agreements, and treaties also belong to the seventh house, along with every form of conflict and competition, from Little League baseball to nuclear war. Thieves belong to the seventh house, and so do enemies the querent knows about, though enemies unknown to the querent are assigned to the twelfth house. Hunting is a seventh house matter, and any person the querent wishes to locate, known or unknown, may be found here as well. In medical divinations, the seventh house represents the physician. Some of the many questions belonging to the seventh house include:

- Does Stanley love me?
- Will this relationship last?
- Is this a good time to propose marriage?

- Should Carol and I form a business partnership?

- Should I sign the contract?

- Will the Packers win the Super Bowl?

- Will India and Pakistan sign a peace treaty?

- Will my company's bid on the project be accepted?

- Would it be to my advantage to file a lawsuit?

- Will the police catch the thief?

- Is next weekend a good time for deer hunting?

- Will I be able to get in contact with Julie again?

The Eighth House

The eighth house traditionally governs death and everything related to it. It was once common for people to ask a geomancer how long they could expect to live and what sort of death they would die, though no ethical geomancer nowadays will answer such a question. As the house of death, the eighth house governs questions about ghosts and all other spiritual entities, and in the Middle Ages and Renaissance it was also used to find out who committed a murder. Magic performed by the querent, or on his or her behalf, belongs to this house, though divination and occult philosophy belong to the ninth. The eighth house also governs questions about circumstances affecting absent or missing persons, and about money or property the querent has loaned to another person. Questions assigned to the eighth house include:

- Should I get life insurance?

- How seriously should I take Bill's threats?

- Is this a good time to make a will?

- Is the house actually haunted?
- Is the magical working I am planning appropriate?
- Is my neighbor's missing daughter all right?
- Will I ever get back the book I loaned to Greg?

The Ninth House

The ninth house traditionally governs long journeys of all kinds, outward and inward. Trips of more than two hundred miles by land, all voyages by water, and air and space travel belong here, but so do religion and spirituality, colleges and universities, adult education, arts, and dream interpretation. Occult philosophy and divination, as distinct from magical practices, also belong here. Questions assigned to the ninth house include:

- Will I be able to go to Germany this summer?
- How congested will the airport be?
- Should I pursue my interest in Pagan religion?
- Will I be able to get into Harvard?
- Is this a good time to go back to school and finish my degree?
- Should I sign up for music lessons, or would I be wasting my time?
- Does the dream I had last night mean anything?
- Should I study geomancy?

The Tenth House

The tenth house traditionally governs the querent's career, reputation, and position in society. It also represents people in positions of authority and the querent's mother. Politics belong here, from the local school board to the United Nations, and so does the state of the weather. Finally, in medical divinations, the tenth house governs the treatment. Questions appropriate to the tenth house include:

- Should I look for a different job?
- Will I get the promotion?
- Will I get along with my new boss?
- Will the county office approve my building permit?
- How is Mom doing these days?
- Will Senator Smith win reelection?
- Should I run for a seat on the school board?
- Will the weather tomorrow be clear and dry?
- Should I get a second opinion on the proposed treatment for my heart condition?

The Eleventh House

The eleventh house traditionally governs friends, associates, promises, sources of help, and the querent's hopes and wishes. It also governs crops from annual plants, and any question that the querent isn't willing to tell the diviner. Questions assigned to the eleventh house include:

- How is my old college buddy Bill doing?
- Will my friend Sally make good on her promise?

- Can I count on the neighborhood association to support me?

- Will I achieve my fondest dream?

- Will I get a good crop of peas this year?

- I don't want to tell you what my question is—can you answer it anyway?

The Twelfth House

The twelfth house traditionally governs the least pleasant parts of life, including restrictions and limitations, debts owed by the querent, imprisonment, anything secret, and enemies the querent doesn't know about. Magic done by another person to harm the querent belongs here. The twelfth house also governs cattle, horses, donkeys, mules, camels, and all wild animals. Questions assigned to the twelfth house include:

- Will I be able to pay my bills next month?

- Will I be sent to prison?

- Is Ruth hiding something from me?

- Is someone at work trying to get me fired?

- Was the poppet in the front yard a joke, or is someone trying to cast a spell on me?

- Is this horse worth buying?

- Will cattle fetch a good price this year?

The geomantic houses follow a subtle but definite logic, and it's a useful exercise to try putting different questions into their proper place in the system until you can identify the house that goes with any given question.

Interpreting the Twelve Houses

Once you've placed the figures in the houses, identify which house corresponds to the question you need to ask, using the lists of house meanings given earlier in this chapter. A question about money, for example, is a second house question; a question about children belongs to the fifth house, and a question about career goes with the tenth house. When you've chosen the house of the quesited, see what figure appears there. That figure gives you the most basic answer to your question; a favorable figure is a positive answer, an unfavorable figure is a negative one.

Three additional factors need to be brought into play, however. First, always interpret the figure in the first house, the significator of the querent. If the significator of the quesited is favorable, but the significator of the querent is not, the reading is saying that the querent will succeed in getting what he or she wants, but will end up regretting it. If the significator of the quesited is unfavorable, but the querent's significator is favorable, it means that the querent will not succeed, but this will turn out to be for the best. The particular figures in the two houses usually offer clues to the details of the situation and its resolution.

The second additional factor to bring into play in house readings is the fourth house, which refers to the end of the matter under discussion. If the figure in the house of the quesited answers the basic question, and the figure in the first house tells how the querent will be affected by it, the figure in the fourth house tells what the final result of the whole situation will be.

The third additional factor to watch in house readings is whether one or both significators *pass* or *spring* to a third house—in other words, whether the same figures are found elsewhere in the chart. If that happens, it means that another factor is involved in the situation. The house to which the significator passes tells you what the additional factor is. For example, if your question is about the querent's career (a tenth house question) but the querent's significator passes to the ninth house as well, this may mean that the querent's career plans may require him or her to get more education, or relocate more than two hundred miles.

Two sample divinations will help make sense of some of these issues.

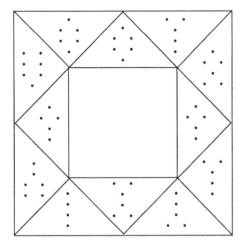

Figure 6-2 Sample Reading 5

In the first example (Figure 6-2), the querent is planning to relocate across the country to go to college, and wants to know what her prospects are. Higher education and a long journey make this a ninth house question twice over, and Caput Draconis in the ninth is a favorable figure for new beginnings. The querent's significator is Puella, also favorable, and passes to the seventh house; this suggests that relationship issues of some sort may be involved in the decision to relocate. The only fly in the ointment is that Caput Draconis passes to the sixth house, the house of illness, where it is an unfavorable figure. The querent would be well-advised to watch her health during and after the move. If she does this, the figure in the fourth house, Conjunctio, suggests that things will work out well in the end.

For the example in Figure 6-3, the querent shares a rented house with several friends, and a new housemate has just moved in. She wants to know whether she and the newcomer will get along. Her significator is Albus, a favorable figure, and it passes to the eleventh house of friends and sources of help. This is a very positive sign. Housemates count as neighbors, to

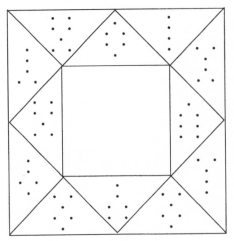

Figure 6-3 Sample Reading 6

the third house is the house of the quesited. The figure there is Acquisitio, and it passes to the fifth house, the house of pleasures and love affairs. This suggests that the querent and her new housemate may get along much better than she expects! The seventh house is not involved, however, and the figure in the fourth house is Fortuna Minor, which represents a factor that begins and ends quickly. Any relationship between them is unlikely to become serious or last long.

Modes of Perfection

Once you've identified the significators of the querent and the quesited and considered their meanings in the houses they occupy, figuring out how they relate to each other is the next step. Certain relationships between the significators, in the language of geomancy, "perfect" the chart; these *modes of perfection* signal that the querent will be able to accomplish his or her goals. Each of the modes of perfection has a name of its own.

Occupation. The first mode is called occupation, and occurs when the two significators have a natural connection to each other. Occupation happens when the same geomantic figure appears in the houses of the querent and the quesited, as shown in Figure 6-4.

The querent hopes to be accepted in a master's degree program, and wants to know her chances. The question, since it has to do with education, is a ninth house matter, and Laetitia appears in both the first and ninth houses. In any question which can be answered by a yes or no, occupation means yes, pure and simple; it is the strongest of all modes of perfection. If (as in this case) a favorable figure appears in both houses, this suggests that the querent will be happy with the outcome of the situation; if they are occupied by an unfavorable figure, the querent will get what he or she wants, but may regret it later.

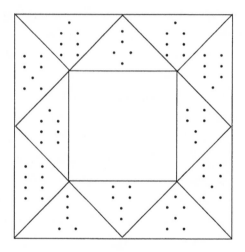

Figure 6-4 Occupation

Conjunction. Nearly as positive an indicator as occupation is conjunction, when one of the significators passes to a house next to the one occupied by the other significator, as in Figure 6-5.

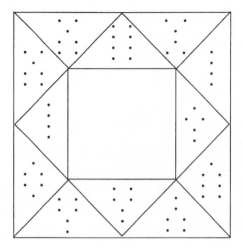

Figure 6-5 Conjunction

Here the querent has quarreled with his business partner and wants to know if the partnership will survive the quarrel. The figure in the first house, the house of the querent, is Via, and the figure in the seventh house, the house of the querent's partner, is Puella. Via also appears in the eighth house, in conjunction with Puella in the seventh, and this suggests that the quarrel can be settled. Traditional lore has it that when the querent's significator passes into a conjunction with that of the quesited, as happens here, the querent will achieve what he or she wants, but will have to work for it. When the significator of the quesited passes into a conjunction with that of the querent, on the other hand, no effort by the querent is needed. Here, this rule would suggest that the querent should be willing to make the first move toward reconciliation.

As always, the meanings of the figures themselves need to be included in the interpretation. Here, in particular, the role of Via is very important. Via always implies change. As the significator of the querent, it suggests that he may have a certain amount of growing and changing to do if the reconciliation is to work.

Mutation. Another positive indicator is mutation, where the significators of the querent and the quesited both pass to neighboring houses elsewhere in the chart, as in Figure 6-6.

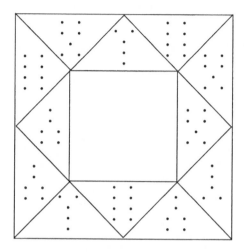

Figure 6-6 Mutation

Here the querent is a candidate for a position in her city government and wants to know if she will win the election. Her significator is Fortuna Minor, which is a good sign to start with, as this is a favorable figure for change. The significator of the quesited, since government is a tenth house mattter, is Caput Draconis, another positive figure, but without a link between the significators this might represent possibilities that remain out of reach.

The link is provided, however, by the mutation between Fortuna Minor in the second house and Caput Draconis in the third. Mutation typically implies that the goal the querent has in mind needs to be sought along unexpected paths, and the house to which the significator of the quesited passes is often a guide to where those paths are to be found. Here the significator of the quesited passes to the third house, which represents the querent's siblings, neighbors, and nearby environment. This suggests that she would be well-advised to pursue a door-to-door campaign and get involved in neighborhood affairs, in order to build the base of support that will win her the position she seeks.

> *Translation.* A fourth positive indicator is translation, where a figure other than the two significators appears in houses next to those of the querent and the quesited, as shown in Figure 6-7.

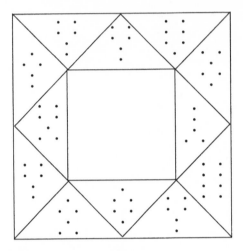

Figure 6-7 Translation

In this example, the querent, who was raised by his mother and stepfather, wants to know if he has any hope of finding his biological father. This is a fourth house question twice over, as it concerns the querent's father and also something hidden, and the initial indications are not good. The querent's significator is Albus, which is a favorable figure but weak, and the significator of the quesited is Carcer, an unfavorable figure meaning limitation and restriction.

What saves this chart is the translation by Fortuna Major in the second and fifth houses. Translation usually means that some outside factor comes into the situation to bring an outcome that the querent cannot

The Art and Practice of Geomancy

manage on his or her own. In this reading, it's clear that while the querent will have little luck finding his father by himself, he may well be able to do so with the help of others; this is reinforced by the fact that Fortuna Major also appears in the eleventh house, the house of friends and sources of help. Local governments or courts may be a particular source of help—this is shown by Fortuna Major also appearing in the tenth house, the house of courts, governments, and people in authority.

The nature of the figure that appears in a translation is of great importance in interpreting its meaning. An unfavorable figure can accomplish a translation just as effectively as a favorable one, but when this happens it often means that the situation will involve some unpleasant experiences before it's resolved. A weak figure such as Albus or Populus, when it carries out a translation, often means that the matter is brought to a conclusion by some unlikely means, or even by what looks like pure coincidence. If the figure that accomplishes the translation represents a person, as it often does, it's possible to get some idea of that person's appearance or personality from the figure.

> *Favorable aspect.* A fifth mode of perfection is favorable aspect, in
> which one significator passes into a positive position in the
> chart relative to the other significator. Aspects, like houses,
> were brought into geomancy from astrological sources, and
> had to be modified to fit the requirements of geomantic
> divination.

The most important modification is that aspects aren't read between the houses of the querent and the quesited. This is a function of the fixed meanings of the houses. The first house is always in a trine aspect, which is favorable, with the fifth and ninth houses, and always in a square aspect, which is unfavorable, with the fourth and tenth; to read these aspects would mean that questions involving children always get a favorable answer, and questions involving real estate always get an unfavorable one!

For this reason, aspects between the significators must involve at least one of them passing to a different house.

Two aspects, sextile and trine, count as modes of perfection in a geomantic chart. The *sextile* aspect in astrology occurs when two planets are at a 60-degree angle to each other; in geomancy, two figures are sextile when there is one house between them. The *trine* aspect in astrology occurs when two planets are at a 120-degree angle to each other; in geomancy, two figures are trine when there are three houses between them.

Table 6-1 lists the houses in aspect to each house in the chart. Note that each house has two houses in sextile aspect and two in trine aspect. One of each is *dexter*, moving against the numerical order of the houses, and the other is *sinister*, moving with the numerical order of the houses. These words, by the way, mean simply "right-hand" and "left-hand," respectively—there's nothing sinister, in the modern sense of this word, about a sinister aspect! Because the dexter aspect breaks with the ordinary flow of the chart, it represents a stronger mode of perfection

Table 6-1: Aspects to Geomantic Houses

House	Dexter Aspects				Sinister Aspects		
	Sextile	Square	Trine	Opposition	Trine	Square	Sextile
1	11	10	9	7	5	4	3
2	12	11	10	8	6	5	4
3	1	12	11	9	7	6	5
4	2	1	12	10	8	7	6
5	3	2	1	11	9	8	7
6	4	3	2	12	10	9	8
7	5	4	3	1	11	10	9
8	6	5	4	2	12	11	10
9	7	6	5	3	1	12	11
10	8	7	6	4	2	1	12
11	9	8	7	5	3	2	1
12	10	9	8	6	4	3	2

The Art and Practice of Geomancy

than a sinister aspect. Perfection by favorable aspect, however, always stands for success through some indirect means, and if favorable and unfavorable aspects both appear in a chart, this often means that the question is still undecided and may go either way.

> *Company of Houses.* Finally, a chart can be perfected through the company of houses, a specific pattern of relationship between pairs of houses. In this pattern, the first and second houses are always paired, the third and fourth, the fifth and sixth, and so on around the chart. It's important to keep this in mind, as it's a common mistake to read company between houses that aren't paired—for instance, between the second and third house, or the tenth and eleventh.

Start by examining the house paired with the house of each of the significators, to see whether company exists between one or both of the significators and the figures in their paired houses.

There are four modes of company: company simple, company demi-simple, company compound, and company capitular. *Company simple* exists when two paired houses share the same figure. *Company demi-simple* exists when two paired houses are occupied by figures ruled by the same planet—for example, if Albus is in the third house and Conjunctio in the fourth, because both of these figures are ruled by Mercury. *Company compound* exists when two paired houses are occupied by opposite figures— that is, if Puer is in the fifth house and Puella is in the sixth; opposite figures are listed in Table 6-2. *Company capitular*, finally, exists when the figures in the paired houses have the same first or Fire line.

When any one of these four forms of company of houses exists between a significator and the figure in its paired house, the figure in the paired house acts like a second significator. If it passes elsewhere in the chart, any translations or aspects it makes count as though the original

Table 6-2 Figures in Company

Company demi-simple exists between:

Figures of Saturn: Carcer, Tristitia, and Cauda Draconis

Figures of Jupiter: Acquisitio, Laetitia, and Caput Draconis

Figures of Mars: Puer, Rubeus, and Cauda Draconis

Figures of the Sun: Fortuna Major and Fortuna Minor

Figures of Venus: Amissio, Puella, and Caput Draconis

Figures of Mercury: Albus and Conjunctio

Figures of the Moon: Populus and Via

Company compound exists between:

Puer and Puella

Amissio and Acquisitio

Albus and Rubeus

Populus and Via

Fortuna Major and Fortuna Minor

Conjunctio and Carcer

Tristitia and Laetitia

Cauda Draconis and Caput Draconis

significator made them. If both significators are in company with the figures in their paired houses, the resulting chart can get extremely busy!

Whenever company of houses exists, this shows that other people take an active role in the situation, and a chart perfected through company means that these other people bring the situation to a favorable conclusion. If the figure in company with the querent's significator perfects the chart, the friends or associates of the querent are in a position to help. If the figure in company with the significator of the quesited perfects the chart, by contrast, someone associated with the quesited holds the key to the question, and the querent should consider trying to contact that person and asking for help. The characteristics of the figure in company with the quesited can be used to get some sense of the appearance, character, and role of the person in question.

Denial of Perfection

Just as the modes of perfection indicate a positive answer, certain other relationships between significators deny perfection to the chart, and signal a negative answer.

> *Impedition.* The most common denial of perfection is impedition, the absence of any relationship between the significators of the querent and the quesited, as shown in Figure 6-8.

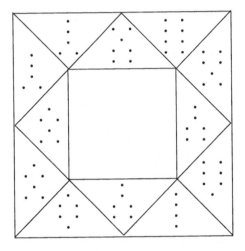

Figure 6-8 Impedition

The querent is interested in starting a sexual relationship with one of her coworkers and wants to know what chance she has of making the relationship happen. Sexuality is a fifth house matter; the querent's significator is Amissio, which is good for love, while that of the quesited is Via, which is an unfavorable figure in many contexts. The critical factor, though, is that the significators are impedited; nothing makes a positive connection between them. Amissio appears in one other place in the chart, the second house; Via appears nowhere else but the fifth, and no third figure interacts with these two and brings the matter to a successful conclusion. Barring favorable Witnesses and Judge, a chart like this gives a negative answer.

> *Unfavorable Aspect.* Just as favorable aspects can perfect a chart, unfavorable aspects can deny perfection. Two aspects, square and opposition, deny perfection in a chart. The *square* aspect in astrology takes place when two planets are at a 90-degree angle to each other; in geomancy, two figures are square when there are two houses between them. *Opposition* in astrology takes place when two planets are at a 180-degree angle to each other, on opposite sides of the sky; in geomancy, two figures are in opposition when there are five houses between them—when, in other words, they are in opposite houses in the chart.

Table 6-1 on page 120 lists the houses in square and opposition to each house in the chart. As with favorable aspects, unfavorable ones aren't read between significators in their own houses; at least one significator must pass to another house to form an aspect. As already mentioned, aspects represent indirect factors bearing on the question. If an unfavorable aspect is the only connection between significators, this usually means that indirect factors are too strong for the querent to overcome. If some mode of perfection connects the significators, but one or more unfavorable aspects also appear in the chart, the unfavorable aspects stand for difficulties that must be overcome; the houses where they appear point to the directions from which these difficulties can be expected to come.

> *Company of Houses.* Where company of houses exists between a significator and the figure in its paired house, this can be a double-edged sword, for an extra significator can make an unfavorable connection just as easily as a favorable one.

Watch especially for unfavorable aspects between the figure in company and the other significator. As mentioned earlier, a figure in company refers to other people in the situation, either friends and associates of the querent (if the figure is in company with the first house) or people associated with the quesited (if the figure is in company with the significator of the quesited). If a figure in company with the querent denies perfection, it often means that the querent's friends and associates are the main obstacle to success. If a figure in company with the quesited denies perfection, on the other hand, this usually means that someone connected with the quesited is the source of trouble.

Additional Methods of Interpretation

The old texts also provide several additional rules for interpreting a chart, which can be combined with the basic rules above to add richness and depth to your divinations.

The Cardines. The first, fourth, seventh, and tenth houses are called the cardines, because they represent the four cardinal directions—east, north, west, and south, respectively. The figures in the cardines have a special influence on the chart. The first house, alongside its other meanings, represents the beginning of the situation. The tenth house represents the middle phases of the situation, the seventh house the conclusion of the situation, and the fourth house its aftermath. The figures in each of these houses should be interpreted according to their own meaning and symbolism, and if any of them pass elsewhere in the chart, any relationships or aspects made between the passing figures and the significators are important.

Look again at Figure 6-4 on page 115. The positive message of the occupation is reinforced by the cardines. Laetitia in the first house represents a hopeful beginning. Puer in the tenth might be favorable or not, depending on context, but Fortuna Major in the seventh and fourth puts the seal of success on the entire reading. The querent clearly has nothing to fear, however challenging the road to the master's program may seem.

> *Combination of figures.* Any pair of figures can be combined,
> using the same process of addition you used to create the
> Nieces, Witnesses, and Judge, to give a snapshot picture of
> their interaction. In Renaissance geomancy, this was stan-
> dard practice, especially for the two significators. If either
> significator was in company of houses, the significator and
> the figure in company with it would be added together to
> divine their relationship, and if a third figure played a role in
> the chart—forming a translation, say—the two significators
> would each be added to it to see how each of them related
> to this third factor.

The new figure produced by the combination of figures shows the current relationship between the two combined figures, and *only* the current relationship. It's not safe to use it as a guide to where that interaction might lead. In a divination about a love affair, for example, a very favorable figure produced by combining the significators of the querent and his or her love interest might simply mean that at the moment, the two are powerfully attracted to one another. Without one of the modes of perfection in the chart, however, that might simply refer to a momentary attraction that ends up going nowhere. In Figure 6-6 on page 117, the significators Fortuna Minor and Caput Draconis combine to produce Puella, but this doesn't ensure that the querent will win the election; it means that at the time of the divination, she wants the position very, very much.

The Reconciler. Traditionally, a figure was made by adding the figure in the first house (the First Mother) to the Judge. This is called the Reconciler. In the old Arabic geomantic manuals, this figure was called the Result of the Result; it shows what the overall outcome of the situation will be. It is particularly useful when the indications of the house chart seem to conflict with what the Judge and Witnesses reveal. As a rule, the Judge and Witnesses define the basic framework of the reading, the house chart shows the details, and the Reconciler sums up how the situation will come out in the end.

Aspects to the significators. This method can yield a snapshot of the balance between positive and negative factors. Simply take every figure in aspect to each of the significators—the two figures in sextile, the two in square, the two in trine, and the one in opposition—and treat them as factors influencing the querent and quesited respectively. The house meanings should not be factored into the interpretation. A favorable figure in a favorable aspect represents a strong positive influence, while a favorable figure in an unfavorable aspect, such as a square or opposition, is weak. An unfavorable figure in an unfavorable aspect, similarly, is a strong negative influence, while an unfavorable figure in a favorable aspect, such as trine or sextile, is weak. Add up all the influences—give +2 for a strong positive, +1 for a weak positive, -1 for a weak negative, and -2 for a strong negative, and simply work out the sum—and you get a good general sense of the situation from the point of view of the querent and quesited respectively.

Projection of points. This can ferret out hidden factors in the
chart. Projection of points is done by counting up the number of single points in the first twelve figures of the chart,
leaving the double points uncounted. Take the total number
of single points and subtract 12; if the result is more than
12, subtract 12 again, and repeat until you have a number
less than 12. If the final number is 0, this stands for the
twelfth house.

The house identified by the projection of points is called the Index,
and represents the hidden factor at work in the situation. In Figure 6-5
on page 116, for example, there are 24 single points in the first twelve
figures; 12 subtracts from this twice with no remainder, so the Index is
the twelfth house. Thus Rubeus in the twelfth house represents the hidden factor in the quarrel between the querent and his lover. The twelfth
house stands for restrictions and limitations, difficult territory for the
passionate energy of Rubeus. This suggests that the querent may feel re-
stricted or limited by the partnership, but has not come to terms with
these feelings. At the same time, Rubeus passes to the eleventh house,
and this suggests that someone in the querent's circle of friends may be
involved in the quarrel in an indirect and unnoticed way.

Part of Fortune. This is similar to the projection of points, but is
found by counting all the points, double as well as single, in
the first twelve figures of the chart, and then subtracting 12
repeatedly until you get a number between 1 and 12. The
Part of Fortune, as the name implies, indicates a house from
which the querent can expect good fortune to come in the
situation. In financial divinations it usually refers to a source
of ready cash.

Putting the Chart Together

It's very common for a geomantic reading to provide a straightforward answer—a clear mode of perfection or a clear denial of perfection, all by itself, with no other factors to confuse the issue. Some charts, on the other hand, challenge the geomancer to weave together complex patterns of meaning pointing in many different directions. This is where geomantic divination becomes an art instead of a mere rule-of-thumb procedure. Each interaction between the significators stands for some part of the total situation, and an experienced geomancer can identify most or all of these factors, assigning them to their place in the overall reading.

The key to this sort of analysis is remembering that the figures aren't simply abstract markers that either do or don't perfect the chart. Each figure has meanings and correspondences of its own, and these can be used to identify the specific person or factor meant by the figure. If a translation, for example, is carried out by Puella, a competent geomancer knows that a woman likely has an important part to play in the situation. If the querent's significator is Tristitia, it's usually wise to see if the problem connects to the querent's feelings of depression or unresolved grief. Every figure that plays an active role in the chart, as a significator, a figure in company, or a figure carrying out a translation, should be interpreted in this way. Figures that pass to another house form an additional source of information that deserves attention.

When a significator, a figure in company with a significator, or a figure involved in a translation passes to a house that's not involved in perfecting the chart (or denying perfection), that figure in that house has a role to play in the reading. In Figure 6-6 on page 117, for example, the querent's significator passes to the fifth house to perfect the chart by mutation, but it also passes to the second house. The second house governs money, and Fortuna Minor represents an interval of success that may not last long. This suggests that the querent will need to spend some money on her campaign for office, but that she should go ahead and spend what she needs to, since the window of opportunity will not be open for long.

Such complex analyses take practice, though, and some old geomantic texts offered tables to help the novice geomancer add up favorable and unfavorable indications to reach a rough yes-or-no answer, when that's all the querent needs to know. The following list, derived from these tables, may be used for this purpose.

To calculate the result of a reading, simply go through the modes of perfection and denial that appear in the chart, note down the numbers assigned to each, and add up separately the numbers assigned to favorable and unfavorable indications. If the total for the favorable indications is larger, the chart is favorable and the answer positive; if the total for unfavorable indications is larger, the opposite is the case.

Table 6-3 Calculating the Indications

Favorable Indications	Unfavorable Indications
Occupation: +5	Impedition: -5
Conjunction: +4	Opposite aspect: -4 per opposition
Mutation: +4	Square aspect: -3 per square
Translation: +4	
Trine aspect: +3 per trine	
Sextile aspect: +3 per sextile	
Company of Houses: Subtract 1 from any relationship or aspect made by a figure in company.	

The Judge and Witnesses from the basic chart, of course, also provide an overall view of the situation. Just as in a shield chart reading, the Judge represents the final outcome of the situation, while the Witnesses stand for the querent (the Right Witness) and quesited (the Left Witness) in general. When these seem to contradict the message given by the significators and their relationship, use a Reconciler made from the figure in the first house and the Judge, and take that as the keynote for the reading.

CHAPTER SEVEN

ADVANCED INTERPRETIVE METHODS

The rules for interpreting geomantic charts given in Chapters Five and Six will meet the requirements of most readings. Certain questions that geomancers are commonly asked, however, call for different methods. Third-party questions, questions with more than two significators, and divinations for direction, location, and time all have methods of their own. Geomancers have also worked out an arsenal of approaches to *special questions*—particular issues that many people once brought to professional diviners for answers and advice. Each special question has rules of its own for determining the answer. The old geomantic texts also include material on how to know when a querent is lying or giving inadequate information, and a system of magical timekeeping, the geomantic hours, with many applications in geomantic divination and magic. All these are covered in this chapter.

Third-Party Questions

The rules for interpreting the geomantic houses covered in Chapter Five, for example, assume that the person asking the question is also the person the question concerns most closely. This is not always the case. Querents—including diviners, of course—frequently want to know about situations involving other people. When the question centers on the querent's relationship with another person, this can be done using the rules already discussed, but what happens when the question deals with some issue in another person's life?

Geomantic lore borrowed an elegant way around this difficulty from horary astrology. When the person central to the divination is not the person receiving (or casting) the divination, the house governing the person central to the divination is treated as the first house, and all other houses change accordingly.

The example in Figure 7-1 will show how this works in practice. The querent's brother is in the military and has been overseas in a combat zone for nearly a year. He is scheduled to finish his tour and return home shortly, and the querent wants to know whether anything will get in the way of his homecoming.

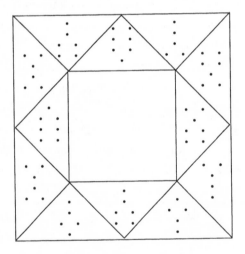

Figure 7-1 Third-Party Question

Fortunately the reading is favorable. For this reading, since the person who is the subject of the divination is the brother of the querent, the significator of the querent is located in the third house, the house of siblings, rather than the first. The significator is Puer, appropriately enough for a soldier. His return home, the subject of the question, is a ninth house matter. Here, though, the house to examine is the ninth house *from the significator of the querent*—the eleventh house of the actual chart. (Count around the chart, starting with the third house as "one," and you'll see how this works.) The eleventh house contains Fortuna Minor. Since Fortuna Minor passes to the fourth house, into a conjunction with the brother's significator, the chart is perfected.

It's worth noting that if this chart had been interpreted in the ordinary way, with the querent's significator in the first house, perfection would have been denied. The figures in the first and ninth houses, Laetitia and Cauda Draconis, have nothing connecting them. This often happens with third-party divinations, and the astute geomancer will always be on the watch for this type of question.

The house that becomes the significator of the querent in third-party questions depends on the relationship between the querent and the person central to the divination.

- **The third house** governs the querent's brothers, sisters, and neighbors.
- **The fourth house** governs the querent's father.
- **The fifth house** governs the querent's own children, and any sexual partners the querent may have outside of a marriage or primary relationship.
- **The sixth house** governs the querent's employees, small animals, and pets.

- **The seventh house** governs the querent's spouse or lover, business partners, open enemies, and also any person with no personal relationship to the querent.

- **The ninth house** governs the querent's teachers.

- **The tenth house** governs the querent's mother, as well as any person with authority over the querent, such as an employer, a judge, or the mayor of the town in which the querent lives.

- **The eleventh house** governs the querent's friends, coworkers, and traveling companions, as well as stepchildren or adopted children.

- **The twelfth house** governs the querent's secret enemies, and horses or other large animals owned by the querent.

More complex relationships can be worked out by combining two or more of these. For example, the querent's grandchild is the child of his or her child. Start from the fifth house for the querent's child, treat that as the first house, then count to the fifth house from there—the ninth house of the chart—and use that as the house of the querent's significator. If the divination is about a lost puppy belonging to the querent's grandchild, take the sixth house (governing pets) from the fifth house (governing children) from the fifth house of the chart—that is, the second house of the chart.

This same process can be used for questions less closely tied to personal relationships. Money or personal property belonging to the querent's spouse, for example, would be the second house from the seventh house, or the eighth house of the chart. If the querent's father is ill, his illness falls in the sixth house from the fourth house, or the ninth house of the chart. If the querent wants to know about income from real estate owned by a business partner, that would belong to the second house (for the income) from the fourth house (for the real estate) from the seventh house (for the business partner)—the twelfth house of the chart.

One common mistake in doing these calculations is to add up the house numbers—adding the fifth house to the fifth house, say, and getting the tenth—rather than counting five houses around the chart from the fifth, which yields the ninth. Try a few examples and you'll discover that using arithmetic will always give you an inaccurate house. Count around the chart, and you'll always end up with the house you need.

Multiple Significators

Some readings require more than two significators. Situations of conflict, in which two or more sides are contending for a single prize, provide a classic example. Many of the old geomantic books used two armies struggling over a castle to illustrate such questions. One significator stood for the querent's army, another for the opposing army, and a third for the castle. From the relationships between these, medieval and Renaissance geomancers not only divined which army would likely end up with the castle, but could offer advice to a commander concerning the tactics most likely to carry the day.

Few modern geomancers will ever need to divine the best way to attack an enemy castle, but other situations of conflict yield readily to the same methods of analysis. The first house represents either the querent or the side the querent supports. The seventh house represents the other side, and the goal of the conflict may be in any other house: for example, the second house for money or personal property; the fourth for real estate, as in actual warfare; the fifth for love, or the sheer fun of the sport; the tenth for honor, fame, political power, or professional advancement, and so on.

The relationships between all three significators need to be studied carefully. Generally speaking, if one side's significator perfects to the significator of the goal and the other does not, the side with the connection will win. The same is the case if one side has a better connection than the other—for instance, if one perfects to the significator of the goal by occupation or conjunction, and the other only by aspects.

If the chart shows a mode of perfection between the two contending sides, this can mean that the struggle results in a tie or is settled peacefully. An occupation linking the two sides often means that the contest results in an alliance or the growth of a friendship; a conjunction often means that the side whose significator passes into the conjunction seeks a settlement or a truce; a mutation often means that both sides decide to settle; a translation suggests that some third party will bring about a resolution. (In this last case, check the aspects of the translating figure to the house governing the goal; if it has a solid link to the goal, and neither of the other significators do, this can mean that someone else will win the competition and leave both sides out of luck!) Finally, if there are no connections linking any of the three significators together, the competition will end in stalemate, or be called off because of some outside factor.

In Figure 7-2, the querent is one of several applicants for a management position in a new Internet company, and she wants to know her chances of getting the position in the face of the competition. Her significator is Albus, in the first house; the other applicants can be lumped together in the seventh, and their significator is Fortuna Minor, while the goal is a tenth house matter and its significator is therefore Laetitia. Neither the querent's significator nor that of the other applicants passes anywhere in the chart; Laetitia, on the other hand, passes to the twelfth house, into conjunction with the querent's significator. It also passes to the fourth house, where it forms a square with both the querent and the other applicants. The querent will get the position, then, but there may be some trouble over the matter—perhaps hard feelings on the part of those who were passed over.

Another piece of traditional lore from the old texts can be applied here. This approach relies on planetary symbolism to show the querent's best strategy in a situation involving conflict, and depends on the figure in the first house. Carcer or Tristitia, which belong to Saturn, suggest an approach based on persistence, patience, and endurance. Acquisitio or Laetitia, figures of Jupiter, suggest relying on powerful friends, support

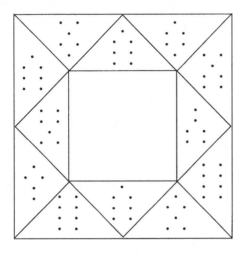

Figure 7-2 Multiple Significators

networks, or financial resources. Puer or Rubeus, belonging to Mars, suggest that the best approach is one of sheer brute force. The figures of the Sun, Fortuna Major or Fortuna Minor, suggest that the querent's own personal qualities will be enough to carry the day. The figures of Venus, Amissio and Puella suggest that tact, gentleness, and a willingness to negotiate will bring success. Albus or Conjunctio, Mercury's figures, suggest an approach based on communication, strategic thinking, and possibly deception. Populus or Via, the Moon's figures, suggest that success will come through responding deftly to the situation as it develops. Caput Draconis indicates that it's too early to say what the proper strategy will be, and Cauda Draconis shows that the situation has already gone too far for any strategy of the querent's to affect it.

In the example in Figure 7-2 above, the querent's significator, Albus, suggests that she should concentrate on making the most of her communications abilities, and think through a plan of action intended to present her as a viable candidate for the new job. The significator of the other applicants, Fortuna Minor, hints that they may not be taking any active steps to pursue the position, and this may well be a major factor in the querent's success.

The method of analysis shown here can be used whenever more than two factors need to be included in a geomantic reading, whether or not conflict is involved. Relationship issues involving more than one person work well with this approach; for example, a querent who is married and also has a lover might ask for a divination in which his significator (in the first house), his wife's (in the seventh house), and his lover's (in the fifth house) all play a role. Similarly, a querent trying to balance a career (in the tenth house) with parenthood (in the fifth house) could get useful advice from a three-significator reading on the subject.

Certain questions require more than three significators, with each house representing a different factor in the issue. The following examples from the old geomantic texts can be used to make sense of these questions.

- *Agriculture.* The first house is the querent, the fourth the land, the fifth perennial or biennial crops, the sixth small livestock, the tenth the weather, the eleventh annual crops, and the twelfth large livestock.

- *Gambling.* The first house is the gambler, the second his or her money, the fifth the game, the seventh the other players, the eighth their money, and the tenth the prize to be won.

- *Health.* The first house is the patient, the sixth the illness, the seventh the physician, and the tenth the medicine or treatment.

- *Real estate.* The first house is the querent, the fourth the property, the seventh the other party, and the tenth the purchase price.

- *Theft.* The first house is the querent, the second the place where the item was stolen, the fourth the place where the item is now, the seventh the thief, and the tenth the police and the court system.

In these charts, the symbolism of the figures in the houses gives you the answer to your question, and so a solid knowledge of the meanings of the figures is crucial. Modes of perfection are less important, though they still have a role—for example, a chart about agriculture that showed the first house perfecting with the eleventh, but not the fifth, would mean that the querent should expect good results from annual crops rather than biennials or perennials.

In a few questions, every house in the chart has its own meaning, and in these readings modes of perfection have no role at all. The most common of these twelve-significator readings are charts for a day, week, month, or some other period of time.

Daily, Weekly, Monthly, and Yearly Charts

One common question put to geomancers in the Middle Ages and Renaissance was how a specified day, week, month, or year would turn out. Charts for this purpose are cast like any other, but once the figures are applied to the houses, different rules apply. Instead of choosing significators for the querent and quesited, all twelve houses are interpreted, and the figure in each house tells how that aspect of the querent's life will unfold during the time period in question. The figure in the first house shows how the querent will fare, the second house what will happen to his money and property, the third the state of his surroundings and neighbors, and so on. When a single figure is shared by two or more houses, this often refers to a single event that affects more than one part of the querent's life.

Figure 7-3 on page 140, for example, shows a reading for a single day. Puella in the first and tenth houses suggests that the querent will start out the day in good spirits, and the weather will be good. Acquisitio in the second promises money or a gift. Carcer in the third and seventh suggests the querent should avoid short journeys and should not try to develop partnerships or long-term relationships that day. Albus in the fourth promises well for the day's end, and if the querent has the chance to spend time with his or her father or to do something relating to real estate or an inheritance, the day favors these. Amissio in the fifth means that amusements will cost more than expected, and gambling is a very bad idea, though as a figure of Venus it promises well for lovemaking. Rubeus in the sixth puts the querent at risk of a feverish illness, and makes this a bad day to hire employees or deal with any of the service professions, as deception is likely. Cauda Draconis in the eighth, ninth, and eleventh could mean that a friend of the querent (eleventh house) living more than two hundred miles away (ninth house) may be in serious trouble (eighth house). Caput Draconis in the twelfth house, finally, means the querent may have to face something he or she fears, but will come through the experience unharmed.

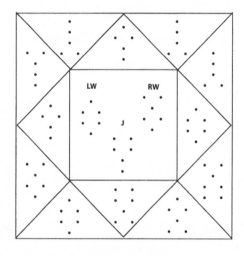

Figure 7-3 Daily Divinations

The Right Witness, Acquisitio, suggests that resources offered on the previous day can be used to meet the challenges of this one. The Left Witness, Carcer, warns that this day's events may put limits on what can

The Art and Practice of Geomancy

be done on the day following. The Judge, Fortuna Major, summing up the day, describes it as a period of swift change caused by outside forces, more fortunate than otherwise, and quickly over.

Divinations for days, weeks, months, and years are popular with querents, but they have another important role as well. Among the very best ways to master the art of geomantic divination is to cast a chart every morning for the day just beginning, interpret it in detail, and then go back the next day and compare the interpretation to what actually happened. This sort of feedback is invaluable in learning how to see the ways the forces diagrammed in a geomantic chart take shape in the realm of everyday human affairs. There is no better way to hone your skills and develop your ability to intuit the meaning of a chart. At the same time, the practical advantages of a daily glimpse into the future are real, and not to be neglected!

Life Readings

The same approach used for daily, weekly, monthly, and yearly readings can also be used for readings intended to explore the favorable and unfavorable influences for an entire lifetime. In the Middle Ages and Renaissance, parents would have such charts cast for their newborn children, and guide the child's upbringing accordingly. People would also have readings of this kind cast for themselves at intervals throughout their lives. It was a commonplace Renaissance thought that a person's destiny could be shaped by their own actions, and so a life reading correct at one point might need revision if the person's choices pointed their destiny in a new direction.

In readings done for a newborn, the first house stands for the querent's personality, the second for his or her economic prospects, the third for his or her schooling, the fourth for his or her father's influence, the fifth for his or her interests and passions, the sixth for his or her health, the seventh for his or her spouse, the eighth for his or her spouse's economic standing, the ninth for his or her higher education and spirituality, the tenth for his or her mother's influence, the eleventh for his or her friends, and the twelfth for his or her weak points. In readings done for an adult, these can be modified along the lines of the house assignments given in Chapter Six.

Finding Directions

Many kinds of questions require the diviner to figure out which direction the querent should go, or which direction the quesited is moving. In the Middle Ages a querent might ask the direction from which an enemy army might arrive, or the route taken by a runaway horse. A modern querent would be more likely to ask where he or she should relocate, or which way a lost pet has gone, but the techniques are the same in either case.

The traditional lore gives two methods for finding directions, and both of them use a slightly different compass than the one most people nowadays are used to. Instead of dividing the compass dial into eight parts—north, northeast, east, southeast, and so on—geomancy divides it into twelve, corresponding to the twelve winds of classical weather lore. Thus the quarter of the compass dial between north and east, say, is divided by two marks, one at north by east (a little more north than northeast) and one at east by north (a little more east than northeast). Keep this in mind, and finding directions by geomancy becomes easy.

Both the traditional methods start by finding the house corresponding to the subject of the reading. If the question is about someone or something other than the querent, choose the house corresponding to that person or thing—a lost pet, for example, would be represented by the figure in the sixth house, a partner or lover by the figure in the seventh, and so on. If the question is about the querent, choose the house corresponding to the querent's motivation in traveling—relocating for college, for example, would be assigned to the ninth house, while relocating as a career move would be the tenth.

For the first method, take the figure in the house corresponding to the subject of the divination and compare it to the list below. This gives you the direction.

- **Puer** is east.
- **Amissio** is south by east (slightly south of southeast).
- **Albus** is north by east (slightly north of northeast).
- **Populus** is north.
- **Fortuna Major** is east by north (slightly east of northeast).
- **Conjunctio** is south by west (slightly south of southwest).
- **Puella** is west.
- **Rubeus** is north by west (slightly north of northwest).
- **Acquisitio** is east by south (slightly east of southeast).
- **Carcer** is south.
- **Tristitia** is west by north (slightly west of northwest).
- **Laetitia** is west by south (slightly west of southwest).
- **Cauda Draconis** is east.
- **Caput Draconis** is west.
- **Fortuna Minor** is east by north (slightly east of northeast).
- **Via** is north.

For the second method, take the figure in the house corresponding to the subject of the divination and see whether it passes to any other house in the chart. If it does, take the number of the house as an indicator of the direction, as shown in the list below. If the figure does not pass to another house, the direction corresponding to the house where it appears is the one indicated by the chart.

- **East:** First house
- **East of southeast:** Twelfth house
- **South of southeast:** Eleventh house
- **South:** Tenth house
- **South of southwest:** Ninth house
- **West of southwest:** Eighth house
- **West:** Seventh house
- **West of northwest:** Sixth house
- **North of northwest:** Fifth house
- **North:** Fourth house
- **North of northeast:** Third house
- **East of northeast:** Second house

If the querent wants to know which direction he or she should travel in order to seek his or her fortune, you can also simply work out the Part of Fortune, using the method explained in Chapter Six. The house where the Part of Fortune appears shows the direction the querent should travel, as shown in the list above, and the figure in that house shows the form of success the querent can expect to find there.

One interesting consequence of the geomantic lore of the directions is that it's possible to do a very effective equivalent of the "other geomancy"—that is, methods of interpreting space and placement, such as feng-shui and vaastu—by casting one or more geomantic charts. If you want to know the best place for a structure on a vacant lot, or want to know the sources of positive or negative influences on a building, simply cast a house chart, and interpret the figures in the twelve houses as indications of the energies in those twelve directions.

Finding Locations

Similar methods can be used to figure out where someone or something is located. One of the most common uses for geomantic divination back in the Middle Ages and Renaissance seems to have been finding lost or stolen items, and the old geomantic texts include detailed methods for working out where an object or a person might be found. Choosing the proper house, once again, is the most important step in this process.

For people, use the list of people corresponding to houses found earlier in this chapter's discussion of third party divinations.

For objects owned by the querent, use the following notes.

- **Second house:** Money, checkbooks, credit cards, and other valuables.

- **Third house:** Newspapers, magazines, letters, instruction manuals, children's schoolbooks, and homework.

- **Fourth house:** Any object not otherwise listed in this table, and any unidentified object.

- **Fifth house:** Clothing, jewelry, dishes, silverware, food and drink, toys and games, and children's belongings.

- **Sixth house:** Tools of all kinds, all tame animals too small to ride, medicines, and anything related to health care.

- **Seventh house:** Wedding rings and contracts.

- **Eighth house:** Wills and anything inherited.

- **Ninth house:** Books, diplomas, and spiritual and religious items.

- **Tenth house:** Legal papers, government and military documents, and weapons.

- **Twelfth house:** Mortgages and paperwork relating to debts, locks and keys, wild animals, and tame animals large enough to ride.

For objects owned by someone other than the querent, the rules for third-party divinations can be used, counting to the relevant house from whatever house governs the other person. In either case, once you have identified the correct house for the person or object the querent wishes to find, the figure in that house shows the kind of place where the person or object is located.

- **Puer** shows that it is outdoors in a park, meadow, or wooded area, or against the outside walls of a house.
- **Amissio** shows that it is in a pasture, a cellar, a basement, a garage, or a stable.
- **Albus** shows that it is located in a barn, a living room, a piece of furniture such as a desk or a chest of drawers, or in an upstairs room.
- **Populus** shows that it is in a laundry room, a place associated with water, or in moving water such as a stream or the sea.
- **Fortuna Major** shows that it is in a rugged or forested area, a government or military building, or some other inaccessible place.
- **Conjunctio** shows that it is in a field, a library or study, or a refrigerator or root cellar.
- **Puella** shows that it is in a bedroom, upstairs room, or attic, in a workshop or factory floor, or on the side of a hill.
- **Rubeus** shows that it is in a garden, orchard, vineyard, kitchen, or pantry.
- **Acquisitio** shows that it is in a high and brightly lit place, indoors or out.
- **Carcer** shows that it is in a shed, storage room, compost heap, or woodshed, or on the ground or floor near a doorway.

- **Tristitia** shows that it is in some underground place, a quarry or other place associated with stone, or in a place with a low ceiling such as an attic or garret.

- **Laetitia** shows that it is in a bathroom, or in stagnant water such as a pond or sump.

- **Cauda Draconis** shows that a person or animal has left the area and will not be found, and an object has been destroyed.

- **Caput Draconis** shows that the object, person, or animal has not actually been lost at all.

- **Fortuna Minor** shows that the object, person, or animal has only been overlooked and will turn up promptly if the querent looks for it more carefully.

- **Via** shows that the object, person, or animal is in motion, and the place where it might be found cannot yet be determined.

For best results, this method can be combined with the second method for finding directions given above. For example, if a wedding ring has gone missing, cast a chart and look in the seventh house. Supposing the figure in this house is Laetitia, and Laetitia also appears in the eleventh house, the querent should look for the ring in a bathroom or other watery place, in a direction south of southeast from where the querent is at the time of the divination.

Calculating Time

The time when a predicted event is likely to happen can also be worked out from a geomantic figure. The old texts include a variety of different techniques for doing this, depending on the exact details that the querent needs to know. The simplest method uses the figure in the house of the quesited to provide a rough estimate. If the figure is Puer, Populus,

Puella, Carcer, or Via, the event will take place within ten days. If the figure is Amissio, Fortuna Major, Rubeus, Tristitia, or Fortuna Minor, the event will take place within five weeks. If the figure is Albus, Conjunctio, Acquisitio, Laetitia, Cauda Draconis, or Caput Draconis, the event will take place within fifteen months.

To narrow down the calculation within these broad limits, check to see if the figure of the quesited passes to another house. If it passes to one of the cardines (the first, fourth, seventh, or tenth houses), or if it does not pass at all and the house of the quesited is one of the cardines, the event will take place in the first third of the time frame defined by the figure—for example, if the figure is Puer, the event will take place within three days or a bit more; if it is Tristitia, within twelve days; if it is Laetitia, within five months. If the figure passes to one of the succeedent houses (the second, fifth, eighth, and eleventh houses) or does not pass at all and the house of the quesited is a succeedent house, the event will take place in the middle third of the time frame defined by the figure. If the figure passes to one of the cadent houses (the third, sixth, ninth, and twelfth houses) or does not pass at all and the house of the quesited is a cadent house, the event will take place in the last third of the time frame defined by the figure.

Another traditional way to calculate time requires a fresh chart, and the question needs to define a unit of time—for example, "How many hours until X happens?" or "How many months will Y last?" Once again, look at the figure of the quesited and compare it to the following list.

- **Puer** is one hundred twenty or seventy-nine.
- **Amissio** is six.
- **Albus** is twelve or five.
- **Populus** is seven or five.
- **Fortuna Major** is sixty-six or fifty-six.
- **Conjunctio** is ten or four.

- **Puella** is eighty-two or six.

- **Rubeus** is nineteen or nine.

- **Acquisitio** is seventy-nine or thirteen.

- **Carcer** is forty-three or thirty.

- **Tristitia** is fifty-eight or thirty.

- **Laetitia** is twenty-five or eleven.

- **Cauda Draconis** is eight or two.

- **Caput Draconis** is eleven or three.

- **Fortuna Minor** is forty-one or one.

- **Via** is five or two.

When the figure of the quesited has more than one number associated with it, look to the favorable or unfavorable state of the chart as a whole—whether the significators perfect, whether favorable or unfavorable figures occupy the cardines, and so on. The interpretation depends on what the querent is hoping for. If he or she wants something to occur quickly, a favorable chart yields the smaller of the two numbers, and an unfavorable chart, the larger; if the querent hopes to put something off as long as possible, the reverse is true.

Another way to fine-tune this or the previous method of time prediction relies on the total number of points in the figures of the chart—the Mothers, Daughters, Nieces, Witnesses, Judge, and Reconciler. Count up the total number of points in these sixteen figures. If the number is ninety-six—the total number of points in the sixteen geomantic figures—the time will be exactly equal to the number predicted by the figure of the quesited. If the number is less than ninety-six, the time will be shorter than the figure predicts, and if more than ninety-six, the time will be longer.

If math doesn't scare you, you can divide the total number of points by ninety-six and multiply that figure by the number predicted by the figure to get a precise measurement. For example, if there are one hundred eight points in the figures of your geomantic chart, the chart is favorable, the figure of the quesited is Fortuna Major, and the querent hopes for a swift conclusion to the subject of the divination, the math works like this:

108 (points in the chart) / 96 = 1.125

56 (Fortuna Major's smaller number) x 1.125 = 63

So, for example, if the querent asked "How many days will pass before I can close the sale of my house?" the answer would be sixty-three days.

A final method of calculating time by geomancy relies on one of the magical dimensions of the art, the lore of the geomantic hours.

The Geomantic Hours

Time plays an important part in the practice of magic, for certain times are more favorable for certain types of magic than others. Medieval and Renaissance magicians paid careful attention to the cycles of time, and recognized that each day and hour corresponded to one of the seven planetary energies. Geomancers during the Renaissance adapted this ancient system of magical timekeeping, part of the occult heritage of ancient Babylonia, to create a system of geomantic hours.

In today's world of precise mechanical timekeeping, the geomantic hours take some getting used to, because they aren't necessarily sixty minutes long. Each geomantic hour in the daytime is one-twelfth of the time between sunrise and sunset, and each geomantic hour in the night is one-twelfth of the time between sunset and sunrise. Since the length of day and night changes constantly through the cycle of the year, and also varies with latitude north or south of the equator, the length of the hours changes constantly; the only two days of the year when all the hours are sixty minutes long are the spring and autumn equinoxes (around March 21 and September 22 each year).

While all this sounds complicated, it's easy to work out the geomantic hours if you know the times of sunrise and sunset, and these can be found in almanacs, astrological ephemerides, and often in your local daily newspaper as well. Four steps will find the length of the geomantic hours on any given day:

Step one: Find the times of sunrise and sunset.

Step two: Figure out the total time from sunrise to sunset in hours and minutes.

Step three: Multiply the number of hours by sixty, and add this to the minutes to give you the total number of minutes between sunrise and sunset.

Step four: Divide the number of minutes by 12 to find the number of minutes in each geomantic hour for that day.

To calculate the number of minutes for a geomantic hour at night, use exactly the same method, but start with the total time from sunset to sunrise the next morning. If you've already worked out the length of the geomantic hours for the previous day, on the other hand, just subtract the number of minutes in the day from 1,440 (the total number of minutes in 24 hours) and divide the result by 12 to find the length of geomantic hours during the night.

While the length of the hours changes during the course of the year, the geomantic figure governing each hour follows a cycle that repeats at one-week intervals. Tables 8-1 and 8-2 give the geomantic figures governing each hour of the day and night for each day of the week, following the traditional charts given in Renaissance geomantic manuals. The cycle follows the more familiar system of planetary hours, but adds an intricate rhythm of its own. Most of the figures rule hours traditionally assigned to their

Table 8-1 Geomantic Hours of the Day

Day:	Sunday	Monday	Tuesday	Wednesday	Thursday	Friday	Saturday
Planet:	Sun	Moon	Mars	Mercury	Jupiter	Venus	Saturn
1	F. Major	Via	Rubeus	Albus	Laetitia	Puella	Tristitia
2	Amissio	Carcer	F. Minor	Populus	Puer	Conjunc.	Acquis.
3	Albus	Laetitia	Puella	Tristitia	F. Minor	Via	Rubeus
4	Populus	Puer	Albus	Laetitia	Amissio	Carcer	F. Major
5	Carcer	F. Major	Via	Puer	Albus	Laetitia	Puella
6	Acquis.	Amissio	Cauda D.	F. Major	Populus	Puer	Conjunc.
7	Rubeus	Albus	Acquis.	Puella	Tristitia	F. Minor	Via
8	F. Minor	Populus	Puer	Conjunc.	Acquis.	Amissio	Carcer
9	Puella	Tristitia	F. Major	Via	Rubeus	Albus	Laetitia
10	Conjunc.	Acquis.	Amissio	Carcer	F. Major	Populus	Puer
11	Via	Rubeus	Conjunc.	Acquis.	Puella	Tristitia	Cauda D.
12	Tristitia	F. Minor	Populus	Rubeus	Conjunc.	Acquis.	Amissio

ruling planets, but Caput and Cauda Draconis, which do not have ruling planets in the usual sense of the term, also have hours assigned to them.

In divination, the geomantic hours provide a relatively precise time measurement, though the system can be difficult to use without casting several charts. If a previous divination shows the day on which an event will take place, a new chart can be cast to find the figure governing the hour in that day, and this will normally narrow things down to one or two possible hours in the day. If a previous divination points out the week, cast one chart to see what planet rules the day on which an event takes place using the planetary ruler of the figure of the quesited, and then cast a second chart to find the figure governing the hour.

The geomantic hours have applications that go well beyond this sort of divination for time. They provide a simple form of divination all by themselves—if you know when an event happened, look up the geomantic hour, and this can be used to give you a basic glimpse into the state of

Table 8-2 Geomantic Hours of the Night

Day:	Sunday	Monday	Tuesday	Wednesday	Thursday	Friday	Saturday
Planet:	Sun	Moon	Mars	Mercury	Jupiter	Venus	Saturn
1	Laetitia	Puella	Tristitia	F. Minor	Via	Rubeus	Albus
2	Puer	Albus	Laetitia	Amissio	Carcer	F. Major	Via
3	F. Major	Via	Rubeus	Albus	Laetitia	Puella	Tristitia
4	Amissio	Cauda D.	F. Major	Populus	Puer	Conjunc.	Acquis.
5	Albus	Laetitia	Puella	Tristitia	F. Minor	Via	Rubeus
6	Populus	Puer	Albus	Acquis.	Amissio	Carcer	Caput D.
7	Carcer	F. Major	Via	Rubeus	Albus	Laetitia	Puella
8	Acquis.	Amissio	Carcer	F. Major	Populus	Puer	Conjunc.
9	Rubeus	Conjunc.	Acquis.	Puella	Tristitia	F. Major	Populus
10	F. Minor	Populus	Cauda D.	Conjunc.	Acquis.	Amissio	Carcer
11	Puella	Carcer	F. Minor	Via	Rubeus	Albus	Laetitia
12	Conjunc.	Caput D.	Amissio	Carcer	F. Major	Populus	Puer

the spiritus mundi during that event. These other, more important applications of the geomantic hours relate to the practice of geomantic magic, and are covered in Chapters Nine and Ten.

Special Questions

The rules already covered in this chapter and the two preceding allow most questions to be answered quickly from a geomantic reading. Over the centuries, however, geomancers worked out handy rules that allow more exact answers to be given to certain questions that are commonly asked by querents. These special questions, as they are called, are listed below by the house that governs the quesited of the question. A chart should be cast specifically for any special question.

Second House

Sources of money: If the querent needs money and wants to know the best way to obtain it, examine the figure in the second house. If this is fortunate and passes to another house, the other house indicates a source of money. If Laetitia is in the second house, for example, and passes to the tenth house, the querent should consider talking to his or her employer about a raise or loan. If the figure in the second house is fortunate but doesn't pass anywhere, it means the querent will have the opportunity to earn the money through his or her ordinary job or business. If the figure in the second house also appears in the first, the querent will get the money in some surprising way, and without having to work for it.

The Index and Part of Fortune, as described in Chapter Six, should always be calculated for money questions. In readings of this sort the Index represents unexpected resources, and the house where it's found can point the querent toward a source of money he or she doesn't expect. The Part of Fortune similarly directs the querent toward opportunities that are likely to pay off.

Third House

Checking news and rumors: The figure in the third house offers one way to determine this. Stable figures suggest that the news report or rumor is true, mobile ones that it is false. The figures Via and Populus have a special message: both of them suggest that the information has become garbled in transmission and is neither wholly true nor completely false.

Another approach to news and rumors is to check the four cardines—the figures in the first, fourth, seventh, and tenth houses. The more of these figures are stable, the more accurate the news or rumors are, while the more of them are mobile, the less accurate.

Judging the quality of advice: Check the tenth house as well as the third. The third house represents the advice, but the tenth house represents the motivation behind the advice. If the figure in the tenth is Rubeus or Cauda Draconis, the person giving you the advice has an ulterior motive, and the advice is not in your best interests.

Quarrels with neighbors, family members, etc.: Pay attention to the figures in the first and third houses whenever a question of this sort is asked. If Cauda Draconis, Tristitia, Carcer, Puer, or Rubeus appears in the first house, the querent wants the quarrel to continue and will resist any attempt to settle it. If any of these signs appear in the third house, the other parties to the quarrel want it to continue and will resist any attempt to settle it. The same principle can be applied to quarrels involving people placed elsewhere in the chart.

Fourth House

Buying or selling real estate: This is one of the questions that require four significators to be interpreted effectively. In questions involving buying and selling real estate, the first house is the querent, the fourth is the property, the seventh is the other party in the transaction, and the tenth is the price. If the querent is buying the property, look for modes of perfection connecting the first house to the fourth to show whether the purchase is accomplished. If the querent is selling real estate, look for modes of perfection connecting the first house to the tenth to show whether the sale goes through. Compare the figures of the first and seventh houses to see which of the parties gets the better of the transaction.

Deciding whether to move: This can be done by casting a chart as though the querent's present home and his or her potential new home were enemies, fighting over the querent. The first house represents the querent, the fourth house is the present home, and the seventh house represents the potential new home. If perfection occurs between the first and fourth but not between the first and seventh, the querent should stay; if it perfects between the first and seventh but not the first and fourth, the querent should move; if it perfects with both, the querent may choose either one with equal benefit; if it perfects with neither, the querent should move, but not to the house he or she has in mind.

Another approach relies simply on the figure in the fourth house. The figures Fortuna Major, Acquisitio, Laetitia, Cauda Draconis, and Caput Draconis are all traditionally favorable for moving. Puer, Amissio, Albus, and Conjunctio are neither favorable nor unfavorable. All other figures are unfavorable for moving.

Finding buried treasure: In the days before modern banks, secret burial was one of the few relatively secure ways to store wealth, and the location of such burials might easily be lost through death or any of the confusions of a troubled age. Archeologists in Europe still turn up old caches of coins and precious metals from the Middle Ages now and then. Few modern geomancers are likely to be so fortunate, but for those interested in experimenting with the method, the following guidelines may be of interest.

The figure in the fourth house has the most to say about the nature and condition of what is buried. Stable figures mean that the buried treasure still exists; mobile figures mean that nothing will be found. Favorable figures indicate that what is buried is something of value, while unfavorable ones promise a worthless find.

Whether the figure in the fourth house passes to another house is also important. A stable figure that does not pass to any other house means that the treasure has not been moved since its burial; one that goes to another house means that something was there once but that it was removed to another place in the past, and it's often possible to guess the place where it was taken by noting the figure and the house to which it passes, and using the meanings discussed above for questions involving location.

Prospecting for minerals: If the chart is perfected in any of the standard ways, minerals exist in the place in question, though the amounts may not be commercially viable. The figure in the fourth house tells what mineral can be found there. Fortuna Major or Fortuna Minor stands for gold or precious stones. Via or Populus predicts silver or some other valuable metal. Carcer or Tristitia suggests gravel, phosphate, building stone, or some other unromantic but commercially useful substance. Puer, Rubeus, or Cauda Draconis predicts some common metal such as iron or zinc. Laetitia, Acquisitio, or Caput Draconis points toward a vein of some rare mineral, such as cadmium or chromium. Puella or Amissio tells of semiprecious stones. Albus or Conjunctio represents energy resources such as oil, coal, natural gas, or uranium.

Lost or stolen objects: If a stable figure appears in the fourth house, the object can be recovered; if a mobile figure, the object is gone for good. The location of the object and whether or not it can be recovered can be determined using the methods for locating things in space or time discussed earlier in this chapter.

Fifth House

Pregnancy: In the days before effective pregnancy tests, geomancers were routinely asked to determine if a woman was pregnant or not. This can be calculated as an ordinary fifth house question. Alternatively, if Acquisitio or Laetitia is in the first, fifth, seventh, or eleventh houses, and neither Puer, Rubeus, Carcer, Tristitia, or Cauda Draconis is in the fifth, this shows pregnancy.

Gender and number of unborn children: If the figure in the fifth house is Populus, Conjunctio, Puella, Rubeus, Carcer, Laetitia, Cauda Draconis, or Via, the child will be a girl; if any other figure, a boy. If Albus, Acquisitio, or Laetitia appears in the fifth, twins are possible.

Luck in gambling: The first house represents the querent, the second his or her money, the fifth the game, and the seventh the other players. If the figure in the first house passes to the fifth, or the figure in the seventh passes to the second, the querent will be fortunate. If the Index is in the second house, this is favorable for gambling, and the same is true if Acquisitio, Laetitia, Albus, or Conjunctio appears in the fifth house. Any other combination of figures predicts that the querent will lose money. Cauda Draconis in the second house indicates that somebody else in the game will cheat the querent.

Sixth House

In the Middle Ages and Renaissance, geomancy played an important role in medical diagnosis and treatment. A number of the old geomantic manuals present rules for diagnosing illness from a geomantic chart, and Robert Fludd wrote an entire treatise on the subject, titled *De Geomantia Morborum (On the Geomancy of Diseases)*. Unless you are a physician or other licensed health care practitioner, you have no business diagnosing illnesses for other people—over and above the ethical issues involved, this is illegal in many jurisdictions—but the traditional rules are worth citing here, since they offer important insights into the art of geomantic interpretation. Questions involving acute illnesses belong to the sixth house; chronic illnesses are discussed under the twelfth house.

Nature of the illness: In the Middle Ages and Renaissance, physicians assigned diseases to the four elements, using rules first devised in ancient Greece. Some conditions are hot and dry, and thus assigned to Fire; some are hot and moist, and assigned to Air; some are cold and moist, and assigned to Water; and some are cold and dry, and assigned to Earth. Conditions of one element can be treated with foods and herbs of the element with the opposite qualities—for example, a head cold with runny phlegm corresponds to water, and can be treated with warming and drying foods such as chicken, and fiery herbs such as ginger and garlic. Finding out the elemental nature of the illness is thus a crucial step in diagnosis and treatment. The outer element of the figure in the sixth house is considered a sure guide to the elemental imbalance behind the illness, and thus to appropriate treatment.

Each of the geomantic figures also corresponds to particular illnesses:

- **Puer** indicates epilepsy, stroke, migraine, or headache.
- **Amissio** indicates sore throat, tonsillitis, and head colds.
- **Albus** indicates illnesses in the hands, arms, and shoulders, and mental illnesses.
- **Populus** and **Via** indicate indigestion, coughs, chest colds, fluid retention, cancer, and illnesses affecting the whole body.
- **Fortuna Major** and **Fortuna Minor** indicate heart disease, burning fevers, upper back trouble, and liver diseases.
- **Conjunctio** indicates colic, diarrhea, and all illnesses of the bowels.
- **Puella** indicates kidney stones, other kidney diseases, and lower back trouble.
- **Rubeus** indicates reproductive system illnesses and sexually transmitted diseases.
- **Acquisitio** indicates hemorrhage, muscular injuries, and epidemic diseases.
- **Carcer** indicates arthritis, bone and joint injuries, and dry skin diseases.
- **Tristitia** indicates depression, nervous troubles, and diseases of the circulation.
- **Laetitia** indicates boils, diseases of the blood, and wet skin diseases.
- **Cauda Draconis** and **Caput Draconis** indicate that the querent's health condition is about to change significantly—for the worse if the figure is Cauda Draconis and for the better if it is Caput Draconis—and treatment will have to respond to the new condition when it arrives.

Location of the illness: Pay attention to where in the chart the figure in the sixth house passes. The first house represents the head, the second house the neck and throat, the third the arms, shoulders, and lungs, the fourth the breasts and stomach, the fifth the heart and upper spine, the sixth the intestines, the seventh the kidneys and lower back, the eighth the genitals and lower spine, the ninth the hips and thighs, the tenth the knees and bones generally, the eleventh the ankles and nervous system, and the twelfth the feet.

It's not accidental that in this system, since every illness appears in the sixth house, the intestines are always involved. One of the basic rules of Renaissance medicine is that every ailment has its roots in one form or another of poor nutrition or digestion.

Seriousness of the illness: This depends on the figures in the first and sixth houses. If these figures perfect by one of the usual modes of perfection or a favorable aspect, the illness will soon be cured. If the significators do not perfect, or perfect by a square or opposition, the illness is likely to be serious. If either one perfects to the tenth house, the house of medicine, the illness will not improve on its own but will respond well to medical treatment.

The quality of the figure in the sixth house also offers information on the time frame of an illness. A stable figure indicates that the querent's present condition of health, whatever that is, will remain for some time to come, while a mobile figure predicts a change for good or ill. Look to the fourth house to find out if the disease is of long standing; a fixed figure there indicates a chronic condition, while a mobile figure represents an illness that has not affected the patient until recently.

Psychosomatic illness: The physicians of the Renaissance were well aware of what we now call psychosomatic illnesses, and geomancy was used to distinguish diseases with mental and emotional roots from those with primarily physical roots, such as infections, poor eating and lifestyle habits, and the like. The figure in the first house governs the spirit, mind, and emotions of the querent. In a chart meant to diagnose an illness, if the figure in the first house is Carcer, Tristitia, Puer, Rubeus, Conjunctio, or Albus, the mental dimension plays a powerful role in the illness, and if the figure in the first house passes into square or opposition with the figure in the sixth, the illness is psychosomatic in nature.

Whether a medical professional or a particular treatment will help: In a chart for an illness, the first house represents the patient, the sixth house the illness, the seventh house the doctor or other medical professional, and the tenth house the medicine or treatment. Look for a mode of perfection connecting the sixth and seventh houses to determine whether a particular doctor or healer will be able to help the patient, and look for a mode of perfection connecting the sixth and tenth houses to determine if a proposed treatment will treat the illness.

Seventh House

Identifying unknown persons: The figure in the seventh house gives the description of any person you don't know. If the figure in this house is in company with the figure in the eighth, this figure can be used to supplement the description.

In a chart cast to identify someone unknown, any house to which the significator of the quesited passes can be read as information about the unknown person. If the figure in the seventh house passes to the tenth, for example, the unknown person has a position of authority; if it passes to the fifth, the unknown person is likely to be a child; if it passes to the eleventh, the unknown person may be a friend of the querent, and so on.

A geomantic chart can also be used to gain hints about the name of an unknown person. Cast a chart specifically for this purpose, and note the figures that appear in the four cardines.

The figure in the first house, according to traditional geomantic lore, gives the first letter of the name; the figures in the tenth and seventh houses give letters in the middle of the name, and the figures in the fourth and fifth houses give letters at the end of the name. If there are two letters listed for a figure, use the letter in boldface if the figure passes elsewhere in the chart, and use the letter in ordinary type if it does not.

- **Puer** is **L** or V.
- **Amissio** is **M** or W.
- **Albus** is D.
- **Populus** is **P** or Y.
- **Fortuna Major** is F.
- **Conjunctio** is **Q** or Z.
- **Puella** is H.
- **Rubeus** is G.
- **Acquisitio** is **I** or S.
- **Carcer** is **O** or R.
- **Tristitia** is B.
- **Laetitia** is **A** or T.
- **Cauda Draconis** is K.
- **Caput Draconis** is C.
- **Fortuna Minor** is E.
- **Via** is **N** or X.

Since most names have more than five letters, a fair amount of intuition can be needed in this form of divination, but the results can be very useful on occasion.

Finding someone: If the querent wishes to find someone, the divination is a seventh house question if the person isn't related to the querent, or is the querent's spouse or partner. Use the appropriate house if the querent is related to the person; the querent's siblings are in the third house, her children in the fifth, her friends in the eleventh, and so on.

If the significator of the quesited passes to any other house in the chart, the house tells where the person can be found. If the figure passes to the fourth house, for example, the person is at home. The sixth suggests a hospital, the tenth the house of the person's parents, the twelfth jail. If it passes to the eighth, the person being sought may be dead. If another figure carries out a translation between the significators, it represents someone with information about the person being sought. Use the symbolism of the figure that carries out the translation to help you identify who has the information.

Lawsuits: Look to the figures in the first and seventh houses. If one of these passes into a favorable aspect with a fortunate figure—that is, trine or sextile aspect to Fortuna Major or Minor, Acquisitio, Laetitia, Puella, Amissio, or Caput Draconis—and the other does not, the one with these aspects will win. If one passes into an unfavorable aspect with an unfortunate figure—that is, square aspect to Carcer, Tristitia, Puer, Rubeus, or Cauda Draconis—and the other does not, the one with these aspects will lose. If both have favorable aspects with fortunate figures, the suit will be settled amicably. If both have unfavorable aspects with unfortunate figures, the suit will turn out badly for both sides. If there are no aspects made at all, some factor will prevent the suit from being heard.

Eighth House

Magical workings: When trying to decide whether a proposed magical working would be favorable for the querent, look to the figure in the eighth house. Puer, Conjunctio, Carcer, Tristitia, Caput Draconis, and Cauda Draconis in this house are favorable for all forms of magic. Via is also favorable for magic, but primarily for astral projection and other workings involving traveling of one sort or another. Fortuna Major, Puella, Acquisitio, and Fortuna Minor, on the other hand, are unfavorable for all magical workings. Rubeus is also unfavorable, as it predicts haste and carelessness. Amissio is favorable for love magic only, and even then the love will not prove lasting; Albus is favorable only for workings to make people happy; Populus is favorable only for magic involving water; and Laetitia is favorable only for clairvoyance and visionary experience.

Ninth House

Problems while traveling: Travelers nowadays face few of the sort of troubles that beset their medieval equivalents, but travel is still not risk-free. If Tristitia appears in the first house, and Rubeus in the second, this is a sign of danger if you are traveling by ship (or by airplane, which involves a similar symbolism). If Conjunctio, Carcer, or Populus appears in the ninth house, you risk encountering thieves. If Rubeus or Puer appears in the sixth and twelfth houses, you face disaster if you travel at all.

Determining whether a dream is significant: Check the figure in the ninth house. A stable figure suggests that the dream is significant, a mobile figure that it means nothing. If a stable figure in the ninth house passes to another house, this points toward the aspect of the querent's life to which the dream relates.

Travel by water: If Cauda Draconis or Rubeus appears in one of the cardines (first, fourth, seventh, or tenth houses) of a geomantic chart about a voyage by water, the ship will not reach its intended port. If these two figures are absent, and fortunate figures such as Laetitia, Fortuna Major, Fortuna Minor, or Caput Draconis appear in any of the cardines, the voyage will be safe and fortunate.

Tenth House

Anticipating the harvest: Gardeners and farmers may ask, as their medieval and Renaissance equivalents did, if the upcoming season promises a good crop or a poor one. Here, both the tenth house, governing the weather, and the fourth house, governing the soil, have to be consulted.

Figures of the elements Air and Water favor agriculture, while figures belonging to Fire and Earth are bad for crops; a fiery figure often means too much heat or too little rain when it appears in the tenth house, and pest problems in the fourth, while an earthy figure often means frosts and cool weather in the tenth and soil deficiencies in the fourth.

If the figures in both these houses favor planting, expect a good yield. If one house has a favorable figure and the other one an unfavorable one, it's often possible to correct the problem and still get a fair crop. If both houses have fiery or earthy figures, on the other hand, the crop is likely to be poor.

Predicting the weather: Even now, with the full armament of modern computers and satellites to draw on, weather prediction is inexact at best, and geomancy may not be useless! Geomantic weather prediction has its roots in ancient and medieval traditions of meteorology far too complex to cover here, but certain basic principles can serve as a starting point.

Use the elements for a first glimpse. In the traditional system, Fire is warm and dry, Water cold and wet, Air warm and wet, and Earth cold and dry. The tenth house of a geomantic chart governs weather, and so the simplest way of forecasting the weather is to cast a chart for the day in question and consider the outer element of the figure that appears in the tenth house. Tristitia, for example, has Earth as its outer element and so means cold and dry weather, though "cold" will of course have a different meaning in July than it has in January, and differences in local climate conditions also have to be taken into account.

The stable and mobile qualities of the figures also offer a way of checking the weather. Here the question is whether the weather on the day of the divination will change by some specified day or time; a mobile figure in the tenth house means yes, a stable one no, and in the former case the element and nature of the figure tells what the change will be.

Finally, the fifth house should always be checked for the likelihood of rain. When the figures in the fifth and tenth houses have the moist elements of Water or Air as their outer elements, rain is certain; if one has Water or Air but the other has Fire or Earth, rain is possible but uncertain; if both have the dry elements of Fire or Earth, count on dry weather.

Eleventh House

Identification of the querent's guardian genius: This Renaissance magical technique relies on the eleventh house, and is explained in detail in Chapter Ten. All other questions relating to the eleventh house can be answered by the normal methods explained in Chapter Six.

Twelfth House

Release from prison: Puer, Amissio, Laetitia, Cauda Draconis, Fortuna Minor, and Via all predict a quick release from prison, while Fortuna Major, Acquisitio, Carcer, and Tristitia all predict a long stay behind bars. The other figures fall in between. If the figure in the first house is stable, this lengthens the stay in prison, while a mobile figure in the first prophesies an early release, especially if it passes to the third or ninth house.

Deceptive Questions

As mentioned back in Chapter Six, sometimes the querent is less than honest with the geomancer. This sometimes happens because the querent feels uncomfortable about some aspect of the question and doesn't want to share all the details. For example, it's not uncommon for young women to ask a diviner "Will I have children?" when what they actually want to know is "Am I pregnant right now?" Similarly, when someone asks "What will my finances be like for the next year?" or some similar question, they're often considering a specific action that would affect their finances—making an investment, leaving a job, or the like.

With practice, you'll learn to read this in the chart itself. When the querent asks about money but the significator of the quesited springs to the fifth house, unless children or love affairs are part of the question, a speculative venture may be at issue. If it springs to the tenth, the querent's career may be at issue, and so on. Certain figures in the first house, though, can offer an additional warning that you may need to be careful in giving any answer at all.

Rubeus, the most important of these figures, represents hidden motives. When it appears as the querent's significator, it can mean that the querent is not being honest with the geomancer. It can also mean that the querent is not being honest with himself or herself. When a question is perfected by occupation, however, with Rubeus in the houses of querent and quesited alike, this usually means the querent is deliberately lying to the geomancer.

Several other figures in the first house warn of similar situations. Amissio in the first house often means that the querent is not providing the geomancer with enough information to interpret the chart accurately. Populus in the first house means that the question the querent has asked is not what he or she actually wants to know; if Populus is in the first and Rubeus is in the eleventh house, the question is fake and the querent is trying to trick the geomancer. If Cauda Draconis is in the first house, the querent has already decided what to do about the situation, and is "shopping around" for a divination that will agree with his or her preconceptions.

You can also check the querent's attitude toward the geomancer by considering the seventh house. In any reading where the querent is not casting his or her own chart, the seventh house represents the geomancer. If the querent's significator passes to the fourth or tenth house, squaring the seventh, or if the querent's significator and the figure in the seventh house both pass to other houses and form an opposite or square aspect, the querent will not take the geomancer's advice. If the querent's significator is

Populus and does one of these two things, the querent has already decided not to take the geomancer's advice, and the reading is a waste of time.

What you should do in readings of this kind depends on the situation. If you are casting a chart for yourself and get one of these combinations, you've been given an opportunity for self-knowledge and a chance to work on the rough edges of your own relationship to geomancy. Take the time to think long and hard about the question you asked and the expectations you placed on it. Learning to cast charts for yourself and interpret the results with the same objective clarity you would use for a stranger's chart is one of the major challenges of geomancy, and confronting your own biases in this way can help you get there.

If you are casting a chart for someone else and one of these patterns appears, you will need to decide what to do depending on the context. If you are divining for a friend, it may be possible for you to point out what the figures say and encourage your friend to be a little more straightforward. If you are divining for a stranger, especially if money is changing hands, it's usually best to end the divination as soon as the pattern appears, give back any money that you may have been paid, and tell the querent that the figure in the first house means the question cannot be answered.

PART THREE

GEOMANTIC MEDITATION
AND MAGIC

CHAPTER EIGHT

GEOMANTIC MEDITATION AND SCRYING

Perhaps the side of geomancy that's received the least attention in recent centuries is its potential as a tool for meditation. For the last hundred years or so, most people in the Western world have thought of meditation as something exotic and Oriental, as though the West had no meditation systems of its own. This is yet another example of the way in which our culture has lost track of its own spiritual roots. The word "meditation" itself comes from the Latin *meditatio*, which, long before geomancy appeared on the scene in the Western world, already stood for powerful methods of inner practice that can stand comparison with any meditative tradition in the world.

It's worth noting, however, that an important difference separates most Western methods of meditation from their Asian equivalents, as well as from recent systems created in the West but based on Eastern models. Although there are exceptions, most Eastern methods of meditation seek to stop the normal flow of thought through the meditator's mind. By fixing the attention on a mantra, a mandala, a breathing pattern, or bare attention itself, these methods empty the mind of content, so that consciousness can return to its sources in the unknown.

The main Western traditions of meditation, by contrast, seek the same goal in a different way. Rather than abolishing thoughts, these methods make the thinking process itself a vehicle for deeper levels of consciousness. By focusing the mind intently on a chosen theme and allowing it to follow that theme through a chain of linked ideas while keeping it from straying, the Western meditator transforms thinking from half-random mental chatter into a powerful and focused way of understanding. At the same time, the knowledge and insight unfolded by this form of meditation often has great value on its own terms.

This kind of meditation is called *discursive meditation*, because it often takes the form of an inner discourse or dialogue. For the last century or so, since the Theosophical Society first popularized Eastern meditative techniques in the West, it's received very little attention in Western occult schools. There's a rich irony here, for discursive meditation was once a core technique of these same schools. Initiates of traditional occult lodges are shown complicated symbolic images during their initiations, and then expected to use discursive meditation on those images to extract the information packed into them.

Tarot decks crafted by the heads of magical orders, for example, usually contain a wealth of magical instruction ready to be decoded and read by discursive meditation. The famous Rider-Waite deck, designed by Golden Dawn initiate Arthur Edward Waite and illustrated by his fellow initiate Pamela Coleman Smith, is bursting at the seams with a wealth of Cabalistic and Hermetic magical lore hardly noticed by tens of thousands of ordinary Tarot readers who simply recognize it as one of the best divination decks around. Alchemy offers the spectacle of an entire esoteric science, taught by symbols, emblems, and allegories, which make no sense at all to a casual glance but can be interpreted readily once the key of discursive meditation is applied.

This makes traditional occult symbolism sound like nothing more than a code meant to keep knowledge out of unauthorized hands. The reality is more complex. The secrets of occult philosophy and practice aren't secret because somebody decided to hide them; they're secret because they can't be understood and used until the person trying to understand and use them has had certain inner experiences, and learned to look at the world in a particular way. Occult symbols such as the Tarot cards and the emblems of alchemy are designed to lead toward those experiences, and point toward that way of looking at the world. When explored and "unpacked" through discursive meditation, these symbols provide keys and insights that allow the occult student to become an initiate in the full sense of the word.

The sixteen geomantic figures are another set of symbols that can be explored in the same way—and have the same useful results. Rooted in the four elements of magical philosophy, and summing up the dance of the elements through the world of human experience, they have powerful lessons to teach when they're approached through the art of discursive meditation. Those lessons apply to the worlds of spirit and everyday life alike, for it's a central teaching of magical lore that the spiritual aspect of reality isn't a faraway realm out of contact with ordinary existence, but the hidden side of ordinary existence itself.

This way of looking at geomancy also has much to teach about the inner dimensions of divination. Each geomantic chart is, in a certain sense, a snapshot of one set of possibilities arising from the dance of the four elements in the anima mundi, and a sense of the dance itself—even if that sense is imperfect, as it may be, and wordless, as it must be—provides the context for every geomantic reading. On a more pragmatic level, meditation on the geomantic figures is perhaps the best of all ways to learn the figures and their symbolism thoroughly, and thus the best way to see to it that the messages of each chart can be opened up, read, and understood.

Preliminaries for Meditation

The key to meditation is learning to enter a state of relaxed concentration. The word "relaxed" needs to be kept in mind here. Too often, what "concentration" suggests to modern people is a kind of inner struggle:

teeth clenched, eyes narrowed, the whole body taut with useless tension. This is the opposite of the state you need to reach. There are three dimensions of meditation—body, breath, and mind, corresponding to the corpus, spiritus, and anima explored back in Chapter One. Excessive tension in any of these dimensions gets in the way of meditation.

For all of the meditation exercises in this chapter, you'll need a place that's quiet and not too brightly lit. It should be private—a room with a door you can shut is best, though if you can't arrange that, a quiet corner and a little forebearance on the part of your housemates will do the job. You'll need a chair with a straight back and a seat at a height that allows you to rest your feet flat on the floor while keeping your thighs level with the ground. You'll need a clock or watch, placed so you can see it easily without moving your head. You'll also need a journal to keep track of your practices, the progress you make with the technique, and any insights you gain as a result of meditating; the journal in which you write down your geomantic divinations can be used for this as well, especially if you're doing a daily geomancy reading, as suggested in Chapter Seven.

Sit on the chair with your feet and knees together or parallel, whichever is most comfortable for you. Your back should be straight but not stiff, your hands resting on your thighs, and your head rising up gently as though a string fastened to the crown of your skull is pulling upward. Your eyes may be open or closed as you prefer; if they're open, they should look ahead of you but not focus on anything in particular. This is the standard position for meditation in Western magical traditions: comfortable, stable, balanced, and a good deal easier on the knees than some Eastern meditation postures.

Preliminary Exercise One

Put yourself in the meditation position, and then spend ten minutes being aware of your physical body. Start at the soles of your feet, your contact point with the Earth, and work your way slowly upward to the crown of your head. Take your time, and notice any tension you feel. Don't try to force yourself to relax; simply be aware of each point of tension. Over time this simple act of awareness will dissolve your body's habitual tensions by bringing them to your attention and revealing the rigid patterns of thought and emotion that form their foundations. Like so much in meditation, though, this process has to unfold at its own pace.

While you're doing this exercise, let your body become as still as possible. You may find yourself wanting to fidget and shift, but resist the temptation. Whenever your body starts itching, cramping, or reacting against stillness in some other way, simply be aware of it, without responding to it. These reactions often become very intrusive during the first month or so of meditation practice, but bear with them. They show you that you're getting past the levels of ordinary awareness. The discomforts you're feeling are actually present in your body all the time; you've simply learned not to notice them. Now that you can perceive them again, you can relax into them and let them go.

Preliminary Exercise Two

Do the first exercise ten minutes daily for two weeks, or until the posture starts to feel comfortable and balanced. After that, it's time to bring in the next dimension of meditation practice: the dimension of breath. As your own body is your link to the level of corpus, your breath is your link to the level of spiritus, because the movement of vital energy through your body is strongly affected by your breathing.

Start this phase of the practice by taking your meditation position and going through the first exercise quickly, as a way of checking in with your physical body and settling into a comfortable and stable position. Then turn your attention to your breath. Draw in a deep breath, and expel it in a series of short puffs through pursed lips, as though you were blowing out a candle.

When every last puff of air is out of your lungs, hold the breath out while counting slowly and steadily from one to four. Then breathe in through your nose, smoothly and evenly, counting from one to four. Hold your breath in, counting from one to four; hold it in by keeping the chest and belly expanded, not by closing your throat. Breathe out through your nose, smoothly and evenly, again counting from one to four. Continue breathing at the same slow steady rhythm, counting in the same way, for ten minutes. The first "puffing" breath is called the cleansing breath, and the rhythmic breath that follows it is called the fourfold breath. Together, they form a safe but effective set of breathing exercises used in many traditional magical schools.

While you're breathing, your thoughts will likely try to stray onto some other topic. Don't let them. Keep your attention on the rhythm of the breathing, the feeling of the air moving into and out of your lungs. Whenever you notice that you're thinking about something else, bring your attention gently back to your breathing. If your thoughts slip away again, bring them back again. With practice, you'll find it increasingly easy to keep your mind centered on the simple process of breathing, and at that point, some of the positive effects of meditation will start to show themselves.

Geomantic Meditation

Do the second preliminary exercise for ten minutes daily for two weeks, or until you start to achieve a state of mental clarity in the fourfold breath. At this point it's time to bring in the third dimension of meditation practice, the dimension of thought, which is your link to the realm of anima. The best way to do this is to proceed to geomantic meditation itself.

Start by selecting what the traditional meditation literature calls a *theme*—that is, an idea or image you want to understand better. Sit down in the meditation posture, and spend a minute or two going through the first preliminary exercises, being aware of your body and its tensions. Then begin the fourfold breath, and continue it for five minutes by the clock. During these first steps, don't think about the theme, or, for that matter, anything else. Simply be aware, first of your body and its tensions, then of the rhythm and pattern of your breathing, and allow your mind to enter into clarity.

After five minutes, change from the fourfold breath to ordinary, slow breathing. Picture the theme in your mind's eye, as though it stood hovering in the air in front of you, and begin thinking about what it means. Recall as many of its aspects and correspondences as you can, and try to see how they relate to one another. Think about the theme in a general way. Then, out of the various thoughts that come to mind as you think about the theme, choose one and follow it out step by step, thinking about its meanings and implications, taking your thoughts as far as you can.

Unless you have quite a bit of experience in meditation, your thoughts will likely wander from the theme again and again. Instead of simply bringing them back in a jump, follow them back through the chain of wandering thoughts until you reach the point where they left the theme. If you're meditating on Puer, for example, and suddenly notice that you're thinking about your grandmother instead, don't simply go back to Puer and start again. Work your way back. What got you thinking about your grandmother? Memories of a Thanksgiving dinner when you were a child. What called up that memory? Recalling the taste of the roasted mixed nuts she used to put out for the guests. Where did that come from? Thinking about squirrels. Why squirrels? Because you heard the scuttling noise of a squirrel running across the roof above you, and it distracted you from thinking about Puer.

Whenever your mind strays from the theme, bring it back up the track of wandering thoughts in this same way. This approach has two advantages. First of all, it has much to teach about the way your mind works, the flow of its thoughts, and the sort of associative leaps it habitually makes. Second, it develops the habit of returning to the theme, and with practice you'll find that your thoughts run back to the theme of your meditations just as enthusiastically as they run away from it. Time and regular practice will shorten the distance they run, until eventually your mind learns to run straight ahead, along the meanings and implications of a theme without veering from it at all.

To start with, spend ten minutes meditating in this way; when this is easy, go up to fifteen minutes, and if you can spare the time, add five more minutes whenever the period you've set yourself seems too easy. When you're done with each session, repeat the cleansing breath once to close the meditation. Write up the experience in your journal as soon as possible afterward. Be sure to note down the images and ideas that came up in the meditation since these are likely to prove useful later, in further meditations or in casting and interpreting geomantic charts.

Geomantic Meditation One

Start out the process by devoting one meditation session to each of the sixteen figures. Begin with Puer, reviewing its section in Chapter Three before starting the meditation. After you finish the fourfold breath and start the meditation itself, start by thinking about as many of Puer's correspondences as you can. Try to get a general sense of the meaning of the figure. In your next meditation session, meditate on Amissio in the same way, and so on through the circle of geomantic figures. This first pass through the figures offers an introduction to the art of geomantic meditation; it helps start the process of getting all sixteen into the deeper levels of the mind, and creates a foundation on which further work can build.

Geomantic Meditation Two

When you've finished the first set of meditations, go back to Puer again, but this time take each of its correspondences as the theme for a separate session of meditation. For every correspondence, ask yourself what this has to teach about the figure, and how it relates to the other factors you've already covered in previous meditations. Some correspondences will make obvious sense, while others may not; in either case, keep working at it during the time you've set aside to meditate on your theme. Even if all you can do is stare blankly at a concept that refuses to offer any insights, the training in focus and mental control is valuable, and few meditation sessions have only that to offer. Like the legendary leprechaun, who surrenders his pot of gold if you keep him in your sight without looking away even once, themes for meditation only surrender their treasures to the steady pressure of the focused mind.

Geomantic Meditation Three

Working your way through all the correspondences of the sixteen geomantic figures will take you around six months if you meditate once a day. (It takes more than three and a half years if you only meditate once a week—a good argument for daily meditation!) By accomplishing this, you'll give yourself a solid grasp of the figures and their meanings, which will pay off richly in divination practice, and will also yield the benefits of regular meditation.

The next step is to meditate on the way the figures combine with one another. Start with Puer as before, and meditate on what happens when you add Puer to each of the figures, starting with itself. Puer plus Puer equals Populus, as you've learned. The question you now need to explore is what this means. Why does the brash boyish energy of Puer, brought together with another expression of itself, turn into the balanced stability of Populus? What does this say about Puer, Populus, and their interaction?

Devote one or more sessions of meditation to this, and then go on to the next combination—Puer and Amissio, which add to form Caput Draconis. What does this teach you about the figures? After one or more sessions on this, go on to add Puer to Albus, and so on around the circle of the figures. When you've worked through all the combinations of Puer, start with Amissio, and combine it with all the figures in turn. Don't hesitate to start by adding it to Puer again—you're likely to find new insights from this combination. When you've worked through all the combinations of Amissio, go on to Albus, and so on through the sixteen figures.

This third set of meditations has obvious value in divination. When you're reading the Judge and Witnesses of a chart, or relating a reconciler to the two figures that gave birth to it, the process gains a wealth of connotation and depth if you've already meditated on that same combination of figures. Still, the rewards of this set of meditations outside divining are at least as substantial. Working through the combinations of the figures is the best way to make the figures themselves living patterns of elemental energy rather than just abstract arrangements of points. From this awareness unfolds the deeper potential of geomancy as a philosophy of the elements and a tool for living in harmony with the living Earth.

The Art of Scrying

Another discipline closely related to meditation is the art of scrying. Scrying originally meant seeing in the ordinary sense—the closely related word "descry," meaning "to sight at a distance," still gets a little use in modern literary English—but "scrying" was adopted many years ago as a term for a very special kind of seeing that doesn't rely on the physical eyes.

To understand scrying, it's necessary to know a little about the magical understanding of consciousness. To most people in the Western world today, consciousness is an odd phenomenon that happens entirely inside the human brain; each consciousness is cut off from all others, except for whatever indirect link can be managed through material means—speech, writing, skin contact, and so on. This notion comes out of the central dogma of modern thought: the claim that everything that's real is material, and that there is nothing in the universe but matter and energy in various states and combinations.

The magical traditions of the Renaissance saw things otherwise. To the Renaissance magician, matter, the realm of corpus, is only a third of reality, and in some ways it's the least important third; the realms of spiritus and anima are indispensible parts of the whole world. The five senses through which we experience the bodies of all things in the world are only one channel by which we can know the world. One of the others is imagination.

Few human capabilities have been as roundly dismissed in our present culture as imagination. To call something imaginary nowadays is to label it as unreal and unimportant. Magicians know, however, that imagination is the most important power human beings have. Imagination is the ability to reshape our experiences into new forms. It's by way of imagination that we assemble the flurry of experiences around us into a world that can be comprehended, and it's by way of imagination that we can reshape that world.

But the core of the magical understanding of imagination is the idea that the world known through imagination is as real as the world known through the physical senses. If you build up an image in your imagination—for example, a geomantic figure—that image is as real in its own realm as a rock or a tree in this one. Similarly, if you see an imaginary form you didn't create—for example, if one of the geomantic figures appears to you in a dream, or while you're studying the figures and staring off into space—what you're perceiving is a reality. A rock you imagine and a rock you kick don't exist in the same realm; in the old language of magic, the imagined rock exists in the spiritus mundi and the physical rock exists in the corpus mundi, but they both exist. Each has effects in its own realm and each has lessons to teach the perceptive mind.

The realm in which imaginary rocks exist has been called by many names. Modern occult writings refer to it as the astral plane. Henri Corbin, a scholar whose researches into the history of esoteric spirituality are centered on the ways people have interacted with this realm, called it the "imaginal realm." For our present purposes, we can use the same terms used already in this book, and call the realm of images the spiritus mundi. When the poet and Golden Dawn initiate William Butler Yeats, in his famous poem "The Second Coming" wrote, "The Second Coming! Hardly are those words out / When a vast image of Spiritus Mundi / Troubles my sight. . .," he drew on his extensive knowledge of the old language of magical philosophy to express his harrowing vision of a world spinning out of control at the end of an age.

There are many different ways to access the images, vast or otherwise, of the spiritus mundi. For most people, the easiest method is scrying, or, to give it its full technical name, *scrying in the spirit vision*. This uses the ordinary imagination, the faculty of daydreams and reveries—the way discursive meditation uses the thinking mind. Like meditation, too, the art of scrying can be usefully turned to the task of opening up the meaning of the geomantic figures.

The same posture and preliminary exercises used for meditation also lay the foundation for scrying. To practice scrying, take the meditation posture, move your awareness through your physical body from the soles of your feet to the top of your head, and clear your mind and the energy channels of your body with five minutes or so of the fourfold breath. Then, imagine yourself facing a door. Marked on the door is a symbol you wish to explore through scrying, such as one of the geomantic figures.

Spend some time making the image of the door as clear as possible. Don't limit yourself to an abstract image or purely visual imagery. See every detail of the door in your mind's eye; sense its weight and texture. If you like, imagine that the door is painted the traditional color of the geomantic figure, and make its metal fittings out of the metal corresponding to its ruling planet; you'll find the correspondences between metals and planets listed later on page 197.

Once the door and the symbol on it have been built up clearly in your mind's eye, picture the door slowly swinging open. Beyond it is a landscape of some sort. Let it take whatever form it wishes, and spend a minute or more letting it take shape in your imagination before going on. Then, slowly and clearly, imagine yourself rising from your chair, walking to the doorway, and passing through it. The door remains open behind you, and if you look back you can see your physical body sitting in the chair. Look around at the realm beyond the door, and allow yourself to notice as many details as you can.

It's traditional, and useful as well, to make an invocation or prayer to a deity at this point, asking to be guided and protected as you explore this part of the spiritus mundi. Depending on your personal beliefs, you can simply invoke the same deity no matter what you're scrying, or you can invoke a god, goddess, or divine aspect appropriate to the figure you're scrying. Ask the deity to send you a guide, and wait for the guide to appear. It may take human, animal, or some other form. Whatever its form, ask it whether it comes in the name of the deity you've invoked, and ask it to repeat the deity's name. If the spiritual tradition you follow has a protective holy symbol—for example, the cross among Christians, the hammer of Thor among Asatruar, or the Awen symbol among Druids—you can trace this in the air between you and the entity who appears and offers to guide you, if you have any suspicions.

Once you're comfortable accepting guidance from the entity, ask it to show you some of the secrets of the figure you're scrying. It will take you on a journey and show you things, and it may also instruct you directly. Ask it any questions you wish, and pay close attention to its answers. Every detail of the landscape around you and every word spoken to you has something to teach. Treat the things you encounter as though they were real, for the entire duration of the scrying.

A certain degree of caution is in order when dealing with the entities you encounter in your scryings. Some of these are honest and will teach you things of value, but others are not and will try to deceive you. Some people find it difficult to think of "imaginary" beings in these terms, but these entities can be as independent of the scryer's will as the people who appear in dreams; they have a life of their own, and can behave in unexpected ways. Treat them with the same courtesy and caution you would use toward strangers in an unfamiliar town.

When the journey or the instruction comes to an end, ask your guide to bring you back to your starting point, thank it for its guidance, and bless it in the name of the deity you invoked earlier. Then return through the doorway, imagine yourself sitting back in the chair where your physical body has been all the while, and then slowly and carefully imagine the door closing. As it closes, concentrate on the thought that no unwanted energies or beings can come into your daily life from the realm of the figure you've been scrying. Use a few cycles of fourfold breath to clear your mind, then use the clearing breath to close the scrying. Write up the experience in your meditation journal as soon as possible, while the details are still fresh in your mind.

You may find yourself a little disoriented at first after scrying, especially the first few times you do it. If so, eating some food will close your visionary senses down and bring you solidly back into your body. Routine activities such as washing the dishes can also help reorient your awareness back to the realm of ordinary experience.

Working with Scrying

Most people find that scrying is best practiced as a supplement to meditation. If you start by practicing the first and second meditations in the previous section, and then go on to scry each of the figures several times in succession, you'll be able to make the most of the scrying experience.

After a successful scrying, you may find yourself wanting to do another scrying the next day, but it's much more useful to take your time and make sense of what you encounter before going on to the next scrying. The best way to unfold the meaning of your scrying experiences is with the familiar tool of discursive meditation. For every session you spend scrying, plan on spending at least three sessions, preferably more, exploring the meaning of the things you saw and heard during the scrying. Review the experience, sorting it out into events, symbols, and information, and then devote one session of meditation to each of these.

For example, if you scried Fortuna Major, and partway through the scrying a lion-headed man took you to the top of a pyramid, showed you a golden snake wrapped around a crystal egg, and told you that Fortuna Major concealed the great secret of alchemy, you could easily spend four sessions of meditation exploring this part of the scrying. The image of the lion-headed man could be the focus of one meditation, the pyramid another, the snake coiled around the egg a third, and the relation between Fortuna Major and alchemy a fourth. How far you pursue each symbol is up to you, but most novice geomancers run out of patience long before the symbols in their scryings run out of wisdom to offer.

This is not to say that everything in a scrying is necessarily a fount of wisdom. One problem faced by beginners in scrying, especially those who don't have a lot of prior experience with meditation, is that stray thoughts and irrelevancies end up being woven into the scrying by the inadequately trained mind. Several months of daily meditation before your first scrying experiences make a good preventive for this sort of trouble, and it also helps if you've taken the time to become thoroughly familiar with the symbolism of the figures, since this will help your awareness tune into the right part of the spiritus mundi.

Still, like a radio signal in which the message is mixed with static, scryings by novice scryers often contain a mix of useful material and random imagery. As you meditate on each scrying, keep an eye out for things that seem clearly out of place. The colors and symbols of the geomantic figure you scryed are good touchstones; when you see these in your scrying, that's a sign that you had good reception, so to speak, while colors and symbols belonging to other figures is a sign that you got plenty of static.

The most important rule for all these practices is summed up in the old Rosicrucian motto, *Festina lente*—"Make haste slowly." Take meditations and scryings at the speed that works for you, and if you ever feel that you need to take more time to be sure you understand something, take it. One symbol that's fully opened up through meditation or one scrying that's thoroughly understood will take you further than dozens of each that you've skimmed over lightly and then forgotten.

Scrying can be a powerful tool for deepening your understanding of the geomantic figures and opening up the hidden potentials of human awareness, but it can also be an opportunity for many different kinds of foolishness, some of them relatively amusing, some a good deal less so. People have made spectacular blunders by blindly trusting information received from scrying and similar practices in a simplemindedly literal way, and in extreme cases—which are rare, but not rare enough—the results have included madness and death.

The best way to avoid these pitfalls is to remember that scryings take place in a world of their own, that of the spiritus mundi, and the information you receive in them may or may not have anything to do with the realm of the corpus mundi where many of us keep our attention most of the time. Remember that the entities you encounter may resort to lies, flattery, or trickery if that is part of their nature, and it's as foolish to trust them unquestioningly, at face value, as it would be to offer the same trust to the first stranger you encounter on the street. Whatever you encounter in scrying should be taken with a grain of salt, and put through the filter of thorough and thoughtful meditation after the scrying is over.

CHAPTER NINE

PRINCIPLES OF GEOMANTIC MAGIC

Most of the material covered in the earlier chapters of this book focuses on the receptive side of geomantic training and practice. The art of divination and the disciplines of geomantic meditation and scrying can teach you to read the currents of subtle influence that move through the spiritus mundi and shape our lives in ways that most people never realize. As you gain the gift of sensing and interpreting these currents, new worlds open up to you and life's challenges become easier to manage.

The receptive side of geomancy, however, is only half the picture. The same currents in the spiritus mundi that can be sensed and interpreted can be harnessed in more active ways. This is the magical side of geomancy.

In this dimension of the geomancer's art, the symbols and concepts of geomancy turn into tools that can be used to make changes in your life and the lives of others who seek your help. Just as the art of medicine doesn't stop with diagnosis, but also includes ways of healing, the geomancers of the Renaissance predicted and interpreted life's challenges for themselves and their clients, but they also provided appropriate remedies for difficult situations using geomantic magic.

At its core, magic is a practical art, a way of making things happen in the world. No aspect of occultism has been so roundly dismissed by the proponents of modern materialist thought as the idea that magical actions can have effects on the universe of everyday experience. Yet the scorn of those who have never studied magic, much less attempted to practice it, is hardly relevant here.

Magic is no more omnipotent than any other human way of shaping the world, and not every magical working succeeds in its aim. Still, successful magical workings are everyday occurrences for those who take the time to learn and practice the art of magic. If you choose to take that path, and put the art of geomantic magic to work in your own life, you'll learn the truth of the matter for yourself quickly enough.

Understanding Geomantic Magic

There are at least two different ways to work with the magical dimensions of geomancy. One of them, far and away the most common one nowadays, simply uses geomantic symbolism as a resource for some other magical system. Since geomancy shares deep connections with the elements, planets, and signs used in most modern magical systems, this sort of fusion is easy to do, and several of the most influential magical systems of the nineteenth and twentieth centuries made use of geomancy in this way. If this form of geomantic magic appeals to you, the details can be found in many of today's occult handbooks, notably those drawing on the teachings of the Hermetic Order of the Golden Dawn, the fountainhead of much of today's magic.

Still, traditional geomantic lore includes its own approach to magic, a way of shaping the subtle dimensions of existence that unfolds from the basic principles of Renaissance occultism. This approach is unfamiliar to most people today—even those who are experienced in other forms of magic—but it works extremely well, and deserves more attention than it has received in the last four hundred years or so. Like geomantic divination, this traditional approach to geomantic magic applies a simple, flexible set of tools in ingenious ways to respond to the possibilities and challenges of everyday life.

The fundamental insight behind geomantic magic is that the sixteen figures represent the basic conditions of human life. Put another way, they are like a palette of colors you can use to paint the different parts of your life. If your life could use more of one particular color, so to speak, you can increase the amount of that color in your palette and change the balance of the painting that is your life. If one of the colors already laid down is not to your taste, on the other hand, you can figure out which color will blend with it to make a new color more suited to the whole painting.

These two metaphors define two essential strategies for geomantic magic. You can invoke the influence of one of the figures in order to activate that influence in your life. For example, if you feel stuck in a rut, you might invoke Via to bring change. You can also figure out which of the figures represents some part of your life that you want to change, and select another figure that, added to the first one, yields the condition you want to bring into your life. For example, if you realize that the thing keeping you stuck in that rut is a tendency to stay locked up inside yourself, a characteristic of Carcer, you might choose to invoke Via because Carcer plus Via equals Conjunctio, the figure of contact and connection. Either approach can work well; you may find it useful to experiment with both, and decide which works best for you.

While the traditional way of geomantic magic differs from modern magic in many points of philosophy and practice, those familiar with the basic rules of modern magic will recognize some common ground. Thus, in traditional and modern magic alike, every magical working needs to have a clearly defined purpose set out in advance. For best results, you should plan on mulling over the purpose of a potential working until you can phrase the whole thing in a single clear sentence that allows for no double meanings or ambiguities.

It's also crucial, for the successful practice of magic, to make sure that the purpose you have in mind is in harmony with the patterns of the macrocosm. It makes no sense to try to work with the currents of the spiritus mundi if those currents are shaping the universe in the opposite direction! This is where divination comes to the assistance of magic; sensing the patterns of the spiritus mundi, after all, is what divination does best. Before you set out to perform geomantic magic for any purpose, then, cast and interpret a chart to see if the working you have in mind is appropriate. If the answer is no, you need to accept that result, and do something else instead.

There is also an inevitable ethical dimension to magic, because every magical action has consequences that affect the magician. In reality, of course, the word "magical" could be left out of this sentence without making it any less true. People in the modern West have so often tended to use magic as a dumping ground for wish-fulfillment fantasies that the reminder may not be out of place here.

Very often, for example, people new to magic set out to use magical means to try to get money without working for it. Much more often than not, if they actually make the attempt, the reverse happens and they end up with less money than they had when they started. This happens because there is only so much money in circulation at any given time, and for one person to get money without working for it, there has to be someone else who works for it without getting it. To make this your magical intention, in other words, is to seek to increase the total amount of economic unfairness in the world, and this will manifest in your life just as much as anyone else's; as the saying goes, what goes around comes around.

Similarly, using magic to kill or hurt another person, or to control someone else's will—most love spells actually seek this, of course—is a very effective way to bring similar patterns of force to bear on your own life. Equally, the same effect in reverse governs the more positive applications of magic. Whatever you try to bring about by magic, be it blessing or curse, affects you as well as your target. Before performing any act of practical magic, therefore, it's critical to think through the consequences and make sure that you are willing to accept them.

Finally, it's important to remember that the universe has its own patterns and purposes, which are not for your personal benefit. In the great scheme of things, the desires and worries that affect any one human life are very little things. According to Renaissance occult philosophy, the entire universe is brimful of life and intelligence, and the Great Chain of Being that spans the levels of existence reaches as far above us as it does below. Our magic needs to take this into account, not least because its power comes to us through those same higher levels of being.

Talismans and Gamahes

To understand traditional geomantic magic, it's worth remembering the points covered in the first chapter of this book. In the Renaissance spiritual philosophy that underlies geomancy, the physical world we inhabit—the corpus mundi—is only one part of a threefold reality. The anima mundi, the consciousness of the world, and the spiritus mundi, the life force of the world, form the inner dimensions of that reality, and everything that exists in the corpus mundi takes shape in these other, deeper dimensions first. Geomantic divination works, according to these teachings, because it catches the shapes of coming events in the anima mundi and spiritus mundi before they manifest in the corpus mundi.

Yet it's also possible to have a more active relationship with the inner side of reality. In Renaissance occult teachings, the patterns that shape the corpus mundi are always present on the inner levels, whether or not they manifest in some particular corner of the physical world. Given the necessary knowledge, these patterns can be drawn down into the corpus mundi and helped to take shape in the world of everyday life. When some part of a querent's life is going badly because one of these patterns is not manifesting there, these methods can make up for the lack and bring positive results.

To turn to an appropriately earthy metaphor, the geomantic mage is like a gardener who realizes that the soil in one part of the garden has become too dry and the plants are wilting. All the gardener needs to solve the problem is a source of clean water, a watering can, and the very simple technical knowledge needed to fill the pot and take the water where it's needed. This is more or less how geomantic magic works. Instead of water, the geomantic "gardener" taps into the influences of the spiritus mundi, and instead of a watering can, he or she uses material forms that resonate with specific patterns in the spiritus mundi.

In traditional geomantic magic, the two most commonly used material forms are called talismans and gamahes. The first of these two gets plenty of use in today's magic, while the second—pronounced "GAH-ma-hey"—is all but unheard of. The irony here is that most of the things modern occultists call talismans would have been considered gamahes four hundred years ago. In the technical language of Renaissance magic, a talisman—also spelled "telesme" in some of the old books—is a material object bearing a picture or figure of some object or being. If the object bears an abstract symbol such as a word, number, or geometrical diagram instead of an image, the mages of the Renaissance called it a gamahe.

In Renaissance terms, for example, if you wanted to call down the influence of the Moon into a material object, you might make a little statue of a woman with bull's horns out of a lunar material such as moonstone or white wax. Alternatively, you might carve a word of power or a geometrical pattern associated with the moon onto some lunar object such as a silver ring. The first of these is a talisman, the second a gamahe.

The lore of Renaissance magic includes many hundreds of images for talismans, and a smaller but still substantial number of words and diagrams for gamahes, relating to almost every conceivable pattern of power in the spiritus mundi. A popular guide to talismans and gamahes such as the *Magical Calendar*, an oversized broadsheet from 1620 packed with occult lore, has images and diagrams relating to the three persons of the Christian trinity, the four elements, the seven planets, the eight Biblical patriarchs, the nine orders of angels, the ten Cabalistic sephiroth, the twelve signs of the Zodiac, the sixteen geomantic figures, and much more. Such major tomes of Renaissance magic as Henry Cornelius Agrippa's *Three Books of Occult Philosophy* list so many patterns for talismans and gamahes that a lifetime would scarcely be long enough to make and use all of them.

Geomantic magic, by contrast, focuses on a much simpler array of images and diagrams, and works with a smaller number of influences. The seven planets and the sixteen geomantic figures make up the tool kit of the geomantic mage. The diagrams used in geomantic gamahes are called the geomantic sigils, and are shown in Figure 9-1 (see pages 194–195). They evolved into standardized forms early in the Renaissance and appear in countless books of magical lore.

To use a geomantic sigil for a gamahe, you simply write or carve one of the sigils of the figure you want to invoke on some material object. Geomantic talismans, on the other hand, require a more creative approach. Renaissance occult lore includes no images for the sixteen geomantic figures, but books such as *Three Books of Occult Philosophy* give instructions for creating images, and these can be followed here. The basic rule is to create a picture that symbolizes what you want to bring about. For example, an image to bring love might show two people embracing, an image to bring courage might show a lion, an image to remove difficulties might show a bird flying away, and so forth. Artistic skill is useful but not necessary for these images; many examples that survive from the Middle Ages and Renaissance are very crudely drawn or carved.

A few traditional tips to personalize the image should be followed. The name of the person, place, or thing you intend to influence with the image should be written on its forehead. The effect you intend to produce should be written on the belly of the figure, if you want to increase something, and on the back of the figure if you intend to decrease something. On the chest of the image, write the name and sigil of the geomantic figure you intend to invoke into it. If you wanted to make a talisman to bring about reconciliation between two people who have quarreled, for instance, you might draw or carve an image of two people shaking hands.

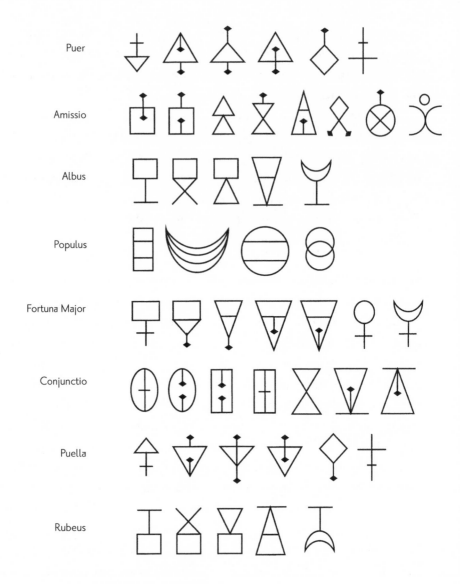

Figure 9-1   The Geomantic Sigils

The Art and Practice of Geomancy

Acquistio

Carcer

Tristitia

Laetitia

Cauda Draconis

Caput Draconis

Fortuna Minor

Via

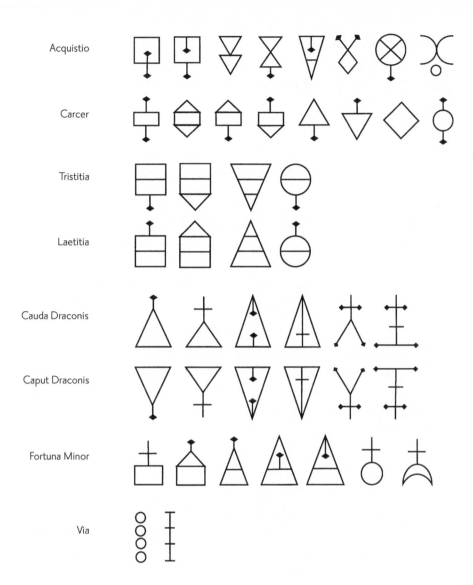

On their foreheads you would write the names of the people whose quarrel you intend to settle; on their bellies you would write the word "reconciliation," and on their chests you would write "Conjunctio" and draw one of the sigils of Conjunctio.

The Materials of Magic

The choice of materials for a talisman or gamahe is just as important as the choice of images or designs, because some substances resonate with the influences of the planets and figures more strongly than others. The art of natural magic, one of the principal branches of Renaissance occultism, amassed a huge body of lore over the centuries, detailing the precise resonances and relationships of literally thousands of material substances. Only a few of these are necessary for the present purpose, however, because the simplicity of geomancy extends all the way to the material basis of its magical work. Metal, wax, or paper, along with the tools to mark them and a small selection of herbs and incenses, will allow you to make a material basis to receive the influences of any geomantic figure.

Metals

Materials for talismans and gamahes vary depending on circumstances and the skills and pocketbook of the magician or the client. The seven metals are considered the best materials to use for talismans and gamahes since they catch and hold the energies of the planets more effectively than any other material substances.

- **Saturn** corresponds to lead.

- **Jupiter** corresponds to tin.

- **Mars** corresponds to iron.

- **Sun** corresponds to gold.

- **Venus** corresponds to copper.

- **Mercury** corresponds to brass.

- **Moon** corresponds to silver.

The planetary metals are well worth using if you can afford them, but gold, at least, is well out of most modern magicians' price range. If you want to use one of the planetary metals, a circle a few inches across can be cut out of a small sheet of the appropriate metal using tin snips, and the image or diagram scratched on it with a sharp tool such as a carbide stylus. Unless you already have experience with engraving, practice on a scrap of metal before you try to do it for magical purposes.

Stones

Metals are not the only effective options for gamahes and talismans; precious and semiprecious stones also saw much use in the Renaissance. The list below includes one or two stones for each planet that can usually be found in rock shops for a reasonable price. When you buy a stone from a dealer, wash it thoroughly in cold running water, dry it, then place it in direct sunlight for at least an hour before using it in any magical working. This removes unwanted influences from it.

- **Saturn** corresponds to jet.

- **Jupiter** corresponds to amethyst or lapis lazuli.

- **Mars** corresponds to beryl or bloodstone.

- **Sun** corresponds to amber or topaz.

- **Venus** corresponds to jade.

- **Mercury** corresponds to tawny agate or chalcedony.

- **Moon** corresponds to moonstone or quartz.

Stones with a flat surface that can have sigils or figures engraved on it are best for making gamahes or talismans. A carbide stylus or some other engraving tool is a must, and so is eye protection—a pair of safety goggles is sufficient. Before you try engraving a sigil or image on stone for magical purposes, practice on an ordinary pebble of the same size and learn how to make your tools do what you want them to do.

Wax

Wax is another good medium for talismans and gamahes. Much easier to handle than metal or stone, it can be melted, cast, carved, molded, and colored as you wish. You can buy blocks of paraffin wax from many grocery stores, while beeswax is available from apiarists and most craft stores; either one will work perfectly well for the purpose. Wax is flammable, so care needs to be taken when melting it; a double boiler is a good investment for this purpose.

If you plan on coloring the wax, follow the instructions that come with the dye you use, or simply get a fresh box of wax crayons, take one or two of the color you want, peel the paper wrapper off, and melt it along with the rest of the wax; this gives a good clear color to plain wax. The following colors are traditional for the planets:

- **Saturn** corresponds to black.

- **Jupiter** corresponds to blue.

- **Mars** corresponds to red.
- **Sun** corresponds to yellow.
- **Venus** corresponds to green.
- **Mercury** corresponds to orange.
- **Moon** corresponds to violet.

Wax gamahes are usually made from plain disks, but wax talismans are often made in three dimensions, like little statues. This takes some practice, and a bit of artistic skill doesn't hurt. In my experience, the best way to make wax figures is to melt the wax, add color and other substances, then pour it into a bowl lined with waxed paper. Wait until it is solid but still warm and flexible, and turn it out onto a sheet of waxed paper. Mold it with your hands into the form you have in mind. If you're making the talisman in a cold room, you may need to work quickly to get it into shape before it hardens.

Paper

Paper is the easiest material to use for geomantic talismans and gamahes, and mages have been using paper (and equivalents such as parchment and papyrus) for these purposes for well over two thousand years. To make a paper talisman or gamahe, simply cut out a circular piece of white or colored paper and draw the image or diagram on it. A drafting compass or a set of circle templates makes tracing out the circle a good deal easier, and a fine-point pen—not a ballpoint, since these tend to skip—with an appropriate color of ink is essential.

The one disadvantage of paper talismans is that they tend to lose their effectiveness over time; paper has no particular resonance with any of the planetary influences, and so the magical charge tends to dissipate after sixty days or so. If the working you have in mind is meant to deal with a short-term situation, though, a paper talisman is usually the best choice.

Paper with Herbal Infusions

You can also get around this limitation of paper by impregnating the paper with a substance that has a strong resonance with one of the planets. One very effective way of doing this starts with a piece of watercolor paper. During the appropriate day and hour, cut out a circular piece of the paper and soak it in a tea or tincture made from an herb corresponding to the planet you plan to invoke.

The most useful herbs for this purpose are given in the list below; all of them can be purchased at most herb stores, online or off. You can buy the herb in bulk and use it to make a strong tea, exactly as though you meant to drink it, or you can purchase a commercially made tincture and use that instead.

- **Saturn** corresponds to horsetail (*Equisetum arvense*).
- **Jupiter** corresponds to lemon balm (*Melissa officinalis*).
- **Mars** corresponds to basil (*Ocimum basilicum*).
- **Sun** corresponds to eyebright (*Euphrasia officinalis*).
- **Venus** corresponds to lady's mantle (*Alchemilla vulgaris*).
- **Mercury** corresponds to fennel (*Foeniculum vulgare*).
- **Moon** corresponds to watercress (*Nasturtium officinale*).

Let the paper dry thoroughly, and then, once again, on the appropriate day and hour draw the image or diagram on it in ink of the appropriate color. This gives you a talisman or gamahe that can be made easily, but has nearly the same lasting effect as one made of metal or stone.

Magic and the Geomantic Hours

Along with the design you choose for a talisman or gamahe and the materials you use, the time when you make it is of critical importance in geomantic magic. One basic rule common to all forms of Renaissance magic, for example, is that magical workings meant to cause increase of any kind should be done during the waxing moon—that is, the time between the new moon and the full, when the visible part of the moon becomes larger with each passing night. Workings meant to cause decrease of any kind, in turn, should be done during the waning moon—that is, the time between the full moon and the new, when the visible part of the moon becomes smaller with each passing night. This rule should be followed in all your geomantic magic.

According to the teachings of Renaissance magic, however, the patterns of the spiritus mundi also change from moment to moment as different planetary influences wax and wane. The lore of the geomantic hours introduced in Chapter Seven can be used to track these influences, so your magical workings can be done when the appropriate influence is strong.

Each day of the week is ruled by one of the seven planets, and each hour of the day is ruled by one of the geomantic figures. When the planet ruling the day also rules the figure of the hour, the power of that planet is very strong, and expresses itself through that figure. Magical workings of that planet done in that hour can tap into the influence of the figure at its strongest, and bind it into a talisman or gamahe at top intensity.

Renaissance magical lore includes a set of special names for the hours of the day and night, as listed in Table 9-1 on page 202. These names remain the same in every day of the week, even though the geomantic figure ruling each hour changes. For example, the hour of Thami (the third hour of the night) on a Monday evening is ruled by Via, but the same hour on a Thursday evening is ruled by Laetitia.

Table 9-1 Magical Names of the Hours

Hours of the Day	Hours of the Night
1. Yayn	1. Beron
2. Janor	2. Barol
3. Nasnia	3. Thami
4. Salla	4. Athar
5. Sadedali	5. Mathon
6. Thamur	6. Rana
7. Ourer	7. Netos
8. Thamic	8. Tafrac
9. Neron	9. Sassur
10. Jayon	10. Aglo
11. Abai	11. Calerva
12. Natalon	12. Salam

The most basic form of magic using the geomantic hours relies on their influence over human affairs. This involves simply timing important actions so that the figure ruling the hour is favorable for the activity you have in mind. If you schedule a wedding during the hour of Conjunctio, mail a job application during the hour of Acquisitio, or do nearly anything during the hour of Fortuna Major, the momentum of time will be in your favor. Even figures that are usually unfavorable can be put to good use in this way. Tristitia is unfavorable in most questions, for example, but if you begin cultivating a garden during the hour of Tristitia, your plants are likely to flourish. The following list indicates the activities favored by each of the geomantic signs.

Favorable Activities for Geomantic Hours

- **Puer** is favorable for any energetic physical activity, such as outdoor recreation, sports of all kinds, and lovemaking.

- **Amissio** is favorable for getting rid of anything, and for any activity that requires spending money without a tangible return, such as making donations to charity, going to parties or restaurants, buying and giving presents, or entertaining. It is also favorable for romance and relationships, and for treating illnesses.

- **Albus** is favorable for any activity of the mind and spirit, such as enrolling in a class, buying books, or engaging in spiritual practice. It is also favorable for investments, business deals, and contracts of all kinds.

- **Populus** is favorable for any activity that depends on popularity or the approval of others, such as politics, public speaking, or seeking favors from people in authority. It is also favorable for dreams.

- **Fortuna Major** is favorable for all activities except those that must be accomplished quickly.

- **Conjunctio** is favorable for any activity that involves making connections, such as communications, trading, or marriage.

- **Puella** is favorable for any emotional or esthetic activity, such as art, music, poetry, or love affairs and relationships.

- **Rubeus** is favorable for any activity that depends on concealment, deception, or hidden knowledge, such as espionage, gambling, or occult sciences. It is also favorable for entertainment and parties, but be prepared for the consequences of excess!

- **Acquisitio** is favorable for any activity aimed at profit or gain of any kind, such as investing, looking for work, or starting a business.

- **Carcer** is favorable for any activity involving isolation and solitude, such as meditation or occult practices, and is also favorable for delay and patience. It is also favorable for anything in which permanence is desired, such as laying a foundation.

- **Tristitia** is favorable for activities related to the Earth, such as building a house, buying or selling real estate, drilling wells, gardening, or planting or harvesting crops. It is also favorable for keeping secrets, and for intellectual, spiritual, and occult pursuits.

- **Laetitia** is favorable for all activities except those that require secrecy.

- **Cauda Draconis** is favorable for endings, departures, and getting out of any difficulty.

- **Caput Draconis** is favorable for beginnings, arrivals, and entering into anything new.

- **Fortuna Minor** is favorable for activities that are finished quickly, such as temporary jobs, short-term investments, or weekend trips.

- **Via** is favorable for activities involving change and movement, such as traveling, moving to a new home, or changing careers.

The most important magical use of the geomantic hours, however, is as a way of timing magical rituals. Whenever you work geomantic magic, do it during the geomantic hour assigned to the figure your working will use, and, if possible, on the day of the figure's ruling planet as well. This is essential to traditional geomantic magic, because the geomantic hours track the currents of the spiritus mundi that give power to your magic, and doing geomantic magic at the wrong time is as useless as trying to turn on an electrical appliance when the current has been shut off. Only when the power is on, to extend the metaphor, can you expect the switch to work, and the table of geomantic hours tells you when power is available.

All the material covered in this chapter—the principles, images, diagrams, materials, and times for geomantic magic—needs to be understood thoroughly before you go on. Once this information has been mastered, you can proceed to the practical dimension of geomantic magic: the consecration of talismans and gamahes and the summit of geomantic magic, the invocation of the guardian genius.

CHAPTER TEN

GEOMANTIC RITUAL MAGIC

The practical application of geomantic magic begins when you recognize a need to bring magical influences into your life or that of someone else, and choose whichever one of the sixteen geomantic figures fits your intention most exactly. In magic as well as divination, each of the figures represents a particular pattern of influence that moves through the spiritus mundi, affecting different areas of human life. In divination, your goal is to sense which combination of figures affects a particular part of the querent's life at a given time. In working magic, by contrast, your goal is to bring the influence of a chosen figure to bear on some part of the querent's life that would benefit from that influence.

The standard geomantic way to bring that influence into action is to create and consecrate a talisman or gamahe. Once you have identified the purpose for your magical working and chosen the figure whose influence you want to bring into the situation, you can assemble the symbolism and materials you need and design a talisman or gamahe that will bring that influence to bear. The final stage—the act of engraving the stone or metal, shaping the wax, or drawing on the paper—is part of the ritual of consecration that brings the talisman or gamahe to life.

Over the last few centuries, a great deal of confusion has gathered around this sort of ritual process. Some people think of ritual as an empty formality, others think of it as a purely psychological tool for concentrating the mind, while still others believe that the ritual all by itself makes the magic happen. The mages and geomancers of the Renaissance, however, had a different view of the matter. To them, ritual was simply a way of entering into deeper resonance with the patterns of the anima mundi and spiritus mundi.

To channel the influences of the Sun as intensely as possible into a gamahe, for instance, they might engrave a solar symbol on a disk of gold on a Sunday at an hour ruled by Fortuna Major, but they would not stop there. The process of engraving the gamahe took place in a chamber draped with yellow cloth, in a magical circle bearing words of power assigned to the Sun, after the magician recited an invocation of the Sun and suffumigated the gamahe—that is, held it in incense smoke—with an incense of the Sun. All these things helped the gamahe, from the moment of its making, resonate as intensely as possible with the patterns of the anima mundi and spiritus mundi it was meant to contain.

Some of the ways that the mages and geomancers of the past did this can be problematic in a modern setting. On the one hand, few modern geomancers can afford the kind of financial outlay that Renaissance mages could, and routinely did, ask their clients to fund. On the other, some of the incense ingredients and other materials given in the old lore are difficult to obtain, ethically inappropriate, or both. Certain changes, then, have had to be made in the methods given here to make them useful to today's geomantic magicians. The principles remain the same, however, and if Pietro di Abano, Christopher Cattan, Robert Fludd, or any other geomancer of the Renaissance made an appearance at a ritual of the sort described in this chapter, they would instantly understand what was going on.

Preparation for Ritual

In order to work geomantic magic using traditional methods, certain requisites have to be present. The first and, in many ways, the most important is a private room where you can be completely undisturbed for an hour or so at a time. If you can set aside a room exclusively for magical purposes, this is a great advantage, but it's not necessary. A spare bedroom, study, or any other private space will do, so long as there's enough room to set up an altar in the center and walk around it in a circle without hitting anything.

For the altar, you can use an endtable, a folding TV tray, or anything else that will put a convenient flat surface near waist height. Once again, if you can set something aside to use exclusively as an altar, this is best, but not required. Near the altar, set a chair—if at all possible, the one you use for meditation. The position of the chair varies depending on the details of the ritual, as explained below.

Put an altar cloth on the altar. The color of the cloth will depend on the planet governing the working you have in mind, so a set of seven cloths in the planetary colors should be on your shopping list before you begin ritual work. Plain rectangles of ordinary cotton broadcloth will be quite sufficient. In some cases, you'll also need a plain piece of white silk to wrap the talisman or gamahe temporarily after the ritual, so this goes on the fabric store shopping list as well.

Other items that go on the altar cloth are four candlesticks, set at the four corners of the altar. Plain brass or pewter candlesticks made to hold tapers are what is needed here. The four tapers may all be white, or they may be in the four traditional elemental colors—red for Fire, yellow for Air, blue for Water, and green for Earth. When you set up the altar, the Fire candle goes in the southeast corner of the altar, the Air candle in the northeast, the Water candle in the northwest, and the Earth candle in the southwest.

This elemental arrangement has an important role in the ritual because each candle represents one line of a geomantic figure, and you will only light the candles corresponding to lines of the figure you work with that have a single point. Thus a ritual working with Fortuna Major would be performed with the northwest and southwest candles lit, representing the single points in the Water and Earth lines of the figure, and the northeast and southeast candles unlit, representing the double points in the Air and Fire lines. Fortuna Minor would be exactly the opposite, with the Fire and Air candles lit and the Water and Earth candles unlit. Laetitia would have only the Fire candle lit; Puella would have the Fire, Air, and Earth candles lit; Via would have all four candles lit, while none of the candles in a Populus ritual would be lit at all.

Besides the candlesticks, you'll need a censer—that is, an incense burner of the sort designed to burn loose incense on charcoal. A simple bowl half full of sand will do the trick, or you can choose one of the ornate censers sold by occult supply shops. A roll or two of self-lighting charcoal will be necessary, and so will the incense itself. Each of the seven planets has its own traditional incenses; you can buy an incense blend for each planet from any good occult supply shop, or use the following simple incenses for the planets:

- **Saturn** corresponds to myrrh.
- **Jupiter** corresponds to cedar.
- **Mars** corresponds to basil.
- **Sun** corresponds to frankincense.
- **Venus** corresponds to rose.
- **Mercury** corresponds to storax (also called amber or liquidambar).
- **Moon** corresponds to jasmine.

Three other things you'll need for the more complex variety of geomantic ritual, as explained later in this chapter, are a cup to hold water, a wand, and a chime or bell. The cup can be made of any material you wish. The wand may be anything from a simple piece of wooden dowel to whatever complicated piece of occult hardware catches your fancy; the chime or bell can be anything that will make clear, distinct chimes when rung. The cup goes on the north side of the altar, the censer on the south, and the wand and chime can be placed anywhere convenient.

You'll need to have some form of clothing set aside exclusively for ritual wear. Most mages use a plain white or black robe, but this is simply a matter of current fashion; anything you find comfortable and convenient will do, so long as you wear it only when performing magical ritual. The reason behind this requirement is the need to keep your ritual space free of any unwanted influence when you consecrate a talisman or gamahe. In the same way that clothes pick up physical dirt, they can pick up unwanted influences in the realms of the anima mundi and spiritus mundi, and these should be kept out of your ritual space.

Before you begin a ritual working to consecrate a talisman or gamahe, a purifying bath is traditional, and this should be done before you put on your ritual garments. If you have a bathtub, clean it, then run a bath and add one-fourth cup of salt, preferably either kosher salt or unbleached sea salt, to the water while the tub fills. If not, use a stoppered sink or a bucket, and give yourself a washcloth bath with the salt water. Have your magical garments with you, along with clean undergarments (if you choose to wear them) and a clean towel and washcloth. Remove all your clothes and bathe your whole body. If you have long hair, you need not dip it in the bath, but a washcloth dipped in the bath water and wrung out should be brushed over your hair to remove unwanted influences. When you are finished, towel off, put on your magical garments, go to your ritual space, and begin the ritual.

Contemplative Ritual

Back in Chapter Four, we saw that preparing for divination can be done in many different ways, some relatively simple, some more complex. The process of consecrating a talisman or gamahe is no different. The two methods presented there, contemplative and theurgic, have their reflections in the magical dimension of geomantic work as well.

To perform the contemplative form of the ritual, have all the tools and materials you need to make your talisman or gamahe in the ritual space before you take your purifying bath. Once the bath is finished, at the beginning of the geomantic hour ruled by the figure you intend to invoke, go into the ritual space, light the incense charcoal and the candles that represent the figure, and put some planetary incense on the charcoal. Sit down in the chair, and enter into meditation. The theme of your meditation is the situation you intend to change using magic, and how it relates to the figure. Focus on how bringing the influence of the figure into the situation will cause the change you have imagined and willed.

When you feel ready, take the tools and materials and make the talisman or gamahe. As you make it, concentrate as intensely as possible on your purpose and the effect you have in mind. When it is finished, put more incense onto the charcoal and hold the talisman or gamahe in the smoke. Concentrate on the idea that the incense smoke and the influence of the geomantic hour are filling the talisman or gamahe with the influence of the figure. Hold that concentration as long and intensely as you can. When your concentration begins to flag, or you feel that the consecration has been firmly accomplished, put out the candles; this completes the ritual.

If the talisman or gamahe is for yourself, take it right away to the place where you need its influence and put it there. For example, talismans and gamahes for prosperity should go in your wallet or another place associated with your financial life; those for healing, dreams, or the like should go under your pillow or mattress, and so on. If it's for someone or something else, and you can get it to its proper place right away, do that. If not, wrap it in a piece of silk cloth and leave it wrapped until you can get it to the person or place that needs it.

Gods, Angels, Intelligences, and Spirits

The more complex form of ritual, the theurgic form, works with the great entities who govern the anima mundi. The complicated cultural and religious history of the Western world gave magicians of the Renaissance two distinct ways to talk about these great beings. On the one hand, Pagan traditions inherited from ancient Rome spoke of those powers as gods, and gave them the images and symbols of the gods and goddesses of classical myth. On the other hand, Christianity inherited from Judaism an extensive body of angel lore, and defined the powers of the anima mundi as angels governing the world as servants of Christianity's solitary god.

Both these approaches remain valid choices in modern geomantic magic, and the distinction between them may be useful for geomancers who want their magic to reflect their personal religious or spiritual beliefs. Pagan geomancers are likely to find it more comfortable to invoke the classical gods and goddesses, while Christian and Jewish geomancers, as well as those who work with Cabalistic magical traditions such as the Hermetic Order of the Golden Dawn, will find the names of the angels more appropriate. Those with flexible religious views may call on both sets of powers; many of the great mages of the Renaissance certainly did so.

Just as so much of geomantic divination borrows principles and practices from astrology, geomantic magic takes its core ideas and methods from planetary magic, the most important branch of the astrological magic of the Middle Ages and Renaissance. The powers of the anima mundi most often invoked in geomantic magic, therefore, are those associated with the seven planets of ancient astrology. Table 10-1 on page 214 outlines the two systems. The names of gods and goddesses are given in their classical Latin form and pronunciation, and those of planetary angels are given in the version used by the mage and geomancer Pietro d'Abano.

Each of the twelve signs of the zodiac has a god and an angel, and these are used in geomantic ritual as well, to call upon the influences of the sign as well as the planet. These are listed in Table 10-2 below, as they appear in the *Magical Calendar* and other standard Renaissance magical sources.

Table 10-1 Gods and Angels of the Planets

Planet	God/dess	Pronunciation	Angel	Pronunciation
Saturn	Saeturnus	sigh-TOOR-noos	Cassiel	CAH-see-ell
Jupiter	Jove	YOH-weh	Sachiel	SAH-khee-ell
Mars	Mavors	MAH-wor-s	Samael	SAH-mah-ell
Sun	Apollo	ah-POH-loh	Michael	MEE-ka-ell
Venus	Venus	WEH-noos	Anael	AH-na-ell
Mercury	Mercurius	mare-CUR-ee-yoos	Raphael	RAH-fa-ell
Moon	Diana	dee-ANN-ah	Gabriel	GAH-bree-ell

Table 10-2 Gods and Angels of the Zodiac

Sign	God/dess	Pronunciation	Angel	Pronunciation
Aries	Athena	ah-THAY-na	Malchidael	mal-KHEE-da-ell
Taurus	Venus	WEH-noos	Asmodel	AZ-moh-dell
Gemini	Apollo	ah-POH-loh	Ambriel	AHM-bree-ell
Cancer	Mercurius	mare-CUR-ee-yoos	Muriel	MOO-ree-ell
Leo	Jupiter	YU-pit-err	Verchiel	VAIR-khee-ell
Virgo	Ceres	KEH-ress	Hamaliel	ha-MALL-ee-ell
Libra	Vulcanus	wool-CAN-oos	Zuriel	ZOO-ree-ell
Scorpio	Mavors	MAH-wor-s	Barbiel	BAR-bee-ell
Sagittarius	Diana	dee-ANN-ah	Adnachiel	ad-NAH-khee-ell
Capricorn	Vesta	WESS-tah	Hanael	HAH-na-ell
Aquarius	Juno	YOO-noh	Gabriel	GAH-bree-ell
Pisces	Neptunus	nep-TOO-noos	Barchiel	BAR-khee-ell

These names play an important part in geomantic magic, but they belong to a level of existence far beyond the elemental world where geomantic magic functions. The planetary spirits reflect the energies of the great planetary powers in the elemental world, and the planetary intelligences provide the link between them. The intelligences and spirits were introduced back in Chapter Four and are listed for convenience here in Table 10-3.

Table 10-3 Geomantic Intelligences and Spirits

Planet	Intelligence	Pronunciation	Spirit	Pronunciation
Saturn	Agiel	AH-gee-ell	Zazel	ZAH-zell
Jupiter	Iophiel	YO-fee-ell	Hismael	HISS-ma-ell
Mars	Graphiel	GRAH-fee-ell	Bartzabel	BART-zah-bell
Sun	Nakhiel	NAH-khee-ell	Sorath	SO-rath
Venus	Hagiel	HAH-gee-ell	Kedemel	KEH-deh-mell
Mercury	Tiriel	TEE-ree-ell	Taphthartharath	taf-THAR-thar-ath
Moon	(see note)	—	Chashmodai	KHASH-mo-die

Note: The Moon has no single intelligence; it has an Intelligence of Intelligences, Malkah be-Tarshishim ve-ad Ruachoth Shechalim (MAHL-kah veh tar-SHISH-im veh-add ROO-akh-oth sheh-KHAL-im), and a Spirit of Spirits, Shad Barshemoth ha-Shartathan (SHAHD bar-SHEM-oth hah SHAR-tah-than). The angel or goddess of the Moon may be invoked instead of these.

The difference between intelligences and spirits needs to be kept in mind in order to work successfully with them. In the simplest terms, intelligences are pure consciousness and dwell in the anima mundi, while spirits are pure energy and dwell in the spiritus mundi. In practice, spirits are blind forces with limited intelligence and no ethical limits. Left to themselves, they will manifest the powers of the planets in unbalanced and uncontrolled ways. This is why the spirits are always summoned, commanded, and released in the names of their intelligences, and the gods or angels of their planets.

The traditional symbolism for each spirit includes, among many other things, a sigil, a gender, an element, several colors, a compass direction, and the power to influence certain aspects of the world of human experience.

- **Zazel** is male and corresponds to the element of Earth. His colors are sapphire blue and black, and his direction is east. An austere, reserved, and silent spirit, he governs time, death, agriculture, building, abstract thought and philosophy, and everything dealing with the past. He is friendly to Taphtharath and an enemy to all the other spirits.

- **Hismael** is male and corresponds to the element of Air. His colors are sea green, purple, and gray, and his direction is northeast. He is calm, placid, and just, and governs good fortune, growth and expansion of all kinds, ceremonies and rites of passage, charities, feasts and entertainments, and advancement in a profession or any organization. He is friendly to Sorath, Kedemel, Taphtharath, and Hasmodai, and an enemy to Zazel and Bartzabel.

- **Bartzabel** is male and corresponds to the element of Fire. His colors are bright red and yellow, and his direction is west. Passionate, temperamental, and forceful, he governs conflicts of all kinds, war, surgery, the removal or demolition of anything, male sexuality, and anything connected with animals. He is friendly to Kedemel and Sorath, and an enemy to Zazel, Hismael, Taphtharath, and Hasmodai.

- **Sorath** is male and corresponds to the element of Fire. His colors are gold and dark red, and his direction is southeast. The mightiest of the spirits, he knows much but speaks little, and governs power of all kinds, leadership, positions of authority, earned success, and all sports and games. He is an enemy to Zazel and Taphtharath, and a friend to Hismael, Bartzabel, Kedemel, and Hasmodai.

- **Kedemel** is female and corresponds to the element of Water. Her colors are white, brown, and green, and her direction is south. A warm and lovely spirit, she governs art, music, dance, social events, all pleasures, love, the emotions generally, and female sexuality. She is friendly to all the spirits except Zazel, who is her enemy.

- **Taphthartharath** is of both genders and corresponds to the element of Water. His/her colors are iridescent rainbow colors, pale gray, and sky blue, and his/her direction is southwest. Nimble, changeable, and cold, this elusive spirit governs learning, messages, communications, all intellectual pursuits, gambling, healing, trade, economics, trickery, deception, and theft. She/he is friendly to Zazel, Hismael, and Kedemel, but an enemy to Bartzabel, Sorath, and Hasmodai.

- **Hasmodai** is female and corresponds to the element of Earth. Her colors are silver and pale yellow, and her direction is north. Gentle, wayward, and the strongest of the spirits after Sorath, she governs travel, change of all kinds, biological cycles, reproduction and childbirth, psychic phenomena, dreams, the unconscious, and the unknown. Her enemies among the spirits are Zazel and Bartzabel; her friends are Hismael, Sorath, Kedemel, and Taphthartharath.

Like geomancy itself, the lore of planetary spirits has its receptive as well as its active dimensions. The theurgic method of preparing for divination is one of these, and you can also use the sigils of the planetary spirits, as given in Chapter Four, for scrying work. This is an effective way to deepen your understanding of the magical dimensions of geomancy. At the same time, of course, the planetary spirits can also be sources of power, for each spirit is a living reservoir of energies that constantly seek expression.

At every moment, for example, Kedemel strives to bring more love and beauty into the world. If a magician performs a working to bring love into a particular situation, and calls on Kedemel in the name of her intelligence Hagiel, the spirit will meet the magician more than halfway. The working becomes an opportunity for Kedemel to fulfill her work in the world, and she will fill it with her energies, as far as the magician's skill and the structure of the working can handle them.

A magician who invoked Zazel for the same purpose, by contrast, would go away empty-handed or worse, because Zazel's energies are opposed to those of Kedemel—as the traditional lore says, the two spirits are enemies. For this reason, it's essential that you take the time to learn the seven planets, their intelligences, and their spirits, and use the right powers for the right purposes. It's also important to learn the following ritual and perform it with due care.

Finally, it deserves to be mentioned here that one spirit not listed in the tables above plays an even more important role in the highest dimensions of geomantic magic than any of the spirits or intelligences of the planets. This is the genius or guardian spirit of the individual geomancer. This aspect of geomantic magic will be covered in the final section of this chapter.

Theurgic Ritual

This ritual draws on traditional Renaissance magical lore, especially as found in the writings of Henry Cornelius Agrippa and the anonymous *Arbatel of Magic*, but has been revised to fit the needs of modern geomancers. Those interested in using strictly Renaissance rituals can find them in the texts cited in the bibliography.

To perform the ritual, have all the tools and materials you need to make your talisman or gamahe in the ritual space before you take your purifying bath, and place the chair so that it faces the direction of the planetary spirit you will be invoking across the altar—for example, if your talisman or gamahe uses a lunar figure and you plan to invoke Hasmodai, put the chair south of the altar, facing across the altar to the north. Once the bath is finished, at the beginning of the geomantic hour ruled by the figure you intend to invoke, go into the ritual space, light the incense charcoal and the candles that represent the figure, and put some planetary incense on the charcoal.

First, stand at the west side of the altar, facing across it to the east. Pause as long as you need to focus your attention on the working you are about to perform. When you are ready, take the wand in your right hand, hold it vertically above the altar, and say, "Procul, O procul esti profani!" (Pronounce this PROH-cool, OH PROH-cool ESS-tee pro-FAH-nee; the words are Latin, and mean "Begone, begone, ye profane ones.")

Second, lower the wand and say the following versicle: "Not in matter did the Fire that is in the First Beyond enclose its active power, but in mind, for the framer of the fiery world is the Mind of Mind." (This passage comes from the *Chaldean Oracles,* a collection of mystical verses that date from Roman times but saw much use in Renaissance magic.) Alternatively, recite the following versicle from Psalm 18: "The Lord is my rock, and my fortress, and my deliverer; my God, my strength in whom I will trust; my buckler, and the horn of my salvation, and my high tower."

Go to the eastern edge of the space. Holding the point of the wand extended outward at chest height, trace a line in the air in a circle around your working space from east to south, to west, to north, and back around again to the east. Imagine that the tip of the wand draws a line of brilliant white light in the air as it passes. When you finish, return to the west of the altar, face east, raise the wand and say, "The circle is traced."

Third, put down the wand. Take up the cup in both hands, and say the following versicle from the *Chaldean Oracles:* "And so therefore first that priest who governeth the works of Fire must sprinkle with the lustral water of the loud-resounding sea." Alternatively, recite the following versicle from Psalm 51: "Cleanse me with a hyssop, O Lord, and I shall be clean; wash me, and I shall be whiter than snow."

Take the cup to the western edge of the space and face west, then circle around the space from west to north, to east, to south, and back around to west, dipping the fingers of your left hand into the water and flicking them outward as you go. When you finish, return to the west of the altar, face east, raise the cup, and say, "The circle is purified."

Fourth, put down the cup, take up the censer, and say the following versicle from the *Chaldean Oracles:* "And when, after all the phantoms are banished, thou shalt see that holy and formless Fire, that Fire which darts and flashes through the hidden depths of the universe—hear thou the voice of Fire." Alternatively, recite the following versicle from Psalm 29: "The voice of the Lord is powerful; the voice of the Lord is full of majesty; the voice of the Lord divideth the flames of fire."

Take the censer to the south, face south, and then circle around the space from south to west, to north, to east, and back again to south. If you have the style of censer that hangs from chains, swing it back and forth as you walk around the circle to cense the boundary of the circle thoroughly. When you finish, return to the west of the altar, face east, raise the censer, and say, "The circle is consecrated."

Fifth, put the censer down. At this point, face the direction of the planetary spirit and recite an invocation of the planetary god or angel whose influence you wish to summon. Two sets of invocations, the Orphic hymns and the Heptameron conjurations, are given in an appendix following this chapter. You may also use an invocation from another source, or create your own. Whichever invocation you choose, imagine as you say it that your ritual space becomes full of the planet's influence and energy. Many people find it helpful to imagine the air around them turning the planet's color as they recite the invocation.

Sixth, sit down in the chair, take up the tools and materials, and make the talisman or gamahe. As you make it, concentrate as intensely as possible on your purpose and the effect you have in mind.

Seventh, when the talisman or gamahe is finished, return to the altar, facing the direction of the spirit, and put more incense onto the charcoal. Hold the talisman or gamahe in the smoke with your left hand. With the wand in your right hand, trace the sigil of the planetary spirit, as though the wand was a paintbrush and you were painting the sigil on the talisman or gamahe.

Eighth, say the following words, inserting the names of the planet, god or angel, intelligence, and spirit where indicated: "In the name of (planetary god or angel), who rules over the influences of (planet), in the name of (zodiacal god or angel), who rules over the influence of (sign of the zodiac) and in the name of your intelligence (intelligence), I conjure you, (spirit), spirit of (planet). Fill this talisman/gamahe with the influences of (planet), and grant it power sufficient to infallibly accomplish the following purpose." State the purpose of the talisman or gamahe. "All this I ask in the great name of (planetary god or angel)."

As you say this, concentrate on the idea that the incense smoke, the influence of the geomantic hour, and the invisible presence of the planetary spirit are filling the talisman or gamahe with magical power. Hold that concentration as long and intensely as you can.

Ninth, wrap the talisman or gamahe in a piece of silk. Say, "I now release any spirits that may have been imprisoned by this ceremony. Depart to your habitations in peace, and peace be between us."

Tenth, take up the cup in both hands, and say the same versicle you used before the purification with water in the opening. Purify with water as in the opening, return to the altar, and say, "The circle is purified."

Eleventh, put down the cup, take up the censer, and say the same versicle you used before the consecration with fire in the opening. Consecrate with fire as in the opening, return to the altar, and say, "The circle is consecrated."

Twelfth, put down the censer, take up the wand, and say the same versicle you said before tracing the circle in the opening. Take the wand to the east, and trace the circle in reverse, going counterclockwise around the circle. As you go, imagine that the tip of the wand is erasing the circle of light you traced in the opening. When you have completed this, return to the west side of the altar and face east. Say, "The circle is traced." Then hold the wand vertically above the altar in your right hand. Say the words "Consummatum est." (Pronounce this CON-sue-MATT-oom EST; this is more Latin, and means "It is completed.") This completes the ritual.

Once again, if the talisman or gamahe is for yourself, take it right away to the place where you need its influence and put it there. For example, talismans and gamahes for prosperity should go in your wallet; those for healing, dreams, or the like should go under your mattress, and so on. If it's for someone or something else, and you can take it at once to its proper place, do that. If not, leave it wrapped in silk until you can get it to the person or place that needs it.

Disposing of Talismans and Gamahes

Talismans and gamahes retain their charge for different lengths of time, depending on the materials used to make them. Paper without an herbal infusion seems to hold a magical charge for one to two months. Wax and herbally infused paper can hold the charge for several years, while metal and stone hold it as long as they remain physically intact. According to some Renaissance texts, certain metal and stone talismans retained their effectiveness for centuries.

If you no longer need the influence of a talisman or gamahe in your life, it needs proper disposal. This is a simple process with paper and wax talismans, since a talisman or gamahe is simply a vessel for the influences of the spiritus mundi, and anything that destroys its material form will release its energies back into the currents of the unseen. Fire is the traditional tool for this purpose, and paper and wax talismans and gamahes can simply be burnt. As you cast them into the flames, thank and release the spirit you invoked in the consecration with words such as these: "In the great name of (planetary god or angel), I thank you, (spirit), servant of (intelligence), for your assistance in this work, and I release you from this (talisman or gamahe). Depart to your habitations in peace, and peace be between us."

Metal and stone talismans and gamahes are a much more difficult matter. A metal talisman or gamahe has to be broken in pieces or, better still, melted, so that no trace of the image or diagram on it remains; this is fairly simple for lead talismans, more challenging for most other metals, and very difficult for iron, which requires very high temperatures to melt. Most stones are even more difficult; jet and amber will burn, and can be disposed of like paper or wax, but most others do not burn and have to be crushed to powder, and the powder thrown into running water. As a general rule, make talismans or gamahes from metal or stone only if you're sure you will want their influence to act for the rest of your life.

Geomancy and the Guardian Genius

The art of making and consecrating talismans and gamahes forms the core practical method of geomantic magic, but there is also a more spiritual dimension to this side of geomancy. This is the art of summoning the guardian spirit or, as it was usually called in Renaissance occult literature, the genius of the individual geomancer.

The word "genius" meant a guardian spirit many centuries before it took on its modern meaning of "very intelligent or talented person." Still, the two concepts are related. In Renaissance tradition, the gifts of intelligence and talent come from the inner dimensions of reality in the form of a guiding spirit. Each person, according to this teaching, receives a genius from the heavens at the moment of birth, and the nature of the genius determines where the newborn child's future talents and skills will be found.

The teachings of Renaissance magic place great stress on figuring out as much as possible about your genius, since the more closely your activities and efforts parallel the gifts of your genius, the more success and happiness you will find in life. The first task in learning to work with your genius is to identify the planet that governs it. Each genius resonates most strongly with one of the seven planets, and even this basic classification can be a most useful source of guidance, because the likes and dislikes of a genius ruled by a given planet follow the friendships and enmities of the planetary spirits.

If your genius is ruled by Mercury, for example, you will find activities of the sort traditionally assigned to Mercury most suited to your talents and temperament, but you will also do well with those of Saturn, Jupiter, and Venus. Those of Mars, the Sun, and the Moon will always be a challenge to you. You could learn this the hard way, by mapping out your successes and failures in life, but you can also figure it out by noticing that Taphthartharath, the planetary spirit of Mercury, is friendly to the spirits Zazel, Hismael, and Kedemel, but an enemy to Bartzabel, Sorath, and Hasmodai.

Old texts present many different ways to calculate the planetary ruler of the genius, most of them based on the natal horoscope, the astrological chart of the heavens at the moment of birth. One common rule was to find out which sign the Moon was in when you were born, take the sign the Moon entered next, and the planet ruling that sign was the one governing your genius. Others said that the most strongly placed planet in the birth chart governs the genius, while still others said that for those born during the day, the planet ruling the sign where the Sun was placed at the moment of birth also ruled the genius, while for those born during the night, the planetary ruler of the sign where the Moon was placed was the ruler of the genius. The rules were so many and varied that Cornelius Agrippa commented despairingly that "it is much difficult to understand the mysteries of the heavens by their directions" (Agrippa 1993, p. 525).

This is another area where the simplicity and directness of geomancy once again comes in handy. The question of what planet rules the genius of the querent is an eleventh house question and can be settled by casting an ordinary chart and seeing what planet rules the figure in the eleventh house. That planet also governs the querent's genius. If Caput or Cauda Draconis appears in the eleventh, the nature of the querent's genius cannot be identified at this time, and you must cast another chart at least two hours later. If any other figure appears there, and the chart perfects, the querent is living in harmony with his or her genius; if the chart does not perfect, the querent is out of harmony with his or her genius and can expect more success and happiness in life by taking the figure in the eleventh as a guide.

This is as far as Renaissance tradition encouraged geomancers to guide querents into the mysteries of the guardian genius. The higher dimension was reserved for serious students of the occult arts. This centered on the process of obtaining conscious contact or, in the language used in some of the old books, the "knowledge and conversation" of the genius. In Renaissance tradition, this was the basis of all the higher dimensions of magic, since a mage's genius can pass on magical secrets directly from the inner realms of existence, protect the mage from physical as well as spiritual dangers, and help the mage interpret the cryptic texts in which advanced magical teachings, then as now, were so often concealed. Like other occult books of the time, geomantic handbooks such as John Heydon's sprawling *Theomagia, or the Temple of Wisdome* included detailed information on the invocation of the genius.

The first step in attaining contact with your genius is learning its name. The name of a spirit isn't simply a convenient label, as personal names are for most people nowadays, but a magical formula that contains the power and presence of the spirit within itself. The occult lore of the Renaissance gave several different methods for finding the name of a genius, most of them even more complex than the methods for finding the planetary ruler of the genius.

Here again, though, geomancy's simplicity offers a straightforward method. Start by finding the planet that governs your genius by casting a chart and identifying the planetary ruler of the figure in the eleventh house, as shown above. Once you have done this, choose an hour governed by that figure, on a day governed by the ruling planet of the figure, when the Moon is waxing. Set up your ritual space as you would for a consecration ritual, with your geomancer's tools on the altar. Before the hour of the figure, take a purifying bath, don your ritual garments, and enter the ritual space as the hour begins.

Open the ritual using either the contemplative or the theurgic method. Burn incense appropriate to the ruling planet of the day and figure. If you wish, recite the Orphic Hymn to the genius or the prayer to the genius from the *Arbatel of Magic* from the appendix, or some other prayer or invocation that seems appropriate to you. Then cast a geomantic chart for the question "What is the name of my genius?"

The key to this chart is the figures in the four cardines. These represent the four aspects of your genius. They can be interpreted as they stand, or used as four Mothers to draw up a new chart that outlines the gifts and powers of the genius in detail. These same four figures, however, also spell out a name of four letters. The figure in the first house gives you the first letter, the figure in the tenth house gives you the second, the figure in the seventh house gives you the third, and the figure in the fourth house gives you the last. The same table of letters given on pages 162 for divinations to find the name of an unknown person should be used here.

You will most likely need to add vowel sounds to the letters that result from this reading to make the name of your genius pronounceable. There are many different methods for doing this. The most convenient one for English-speaking geomancers was developed by British occultists in the eighteenth and nineteenth centuries. The following rules explain how this method works.

- First, the vowels A, E, I, and O, when they appear in a name, are pronounced "ah," "eh," "ee," and "oh," respectively. The letter V, when it appears between two consonants, is pronounced "oo."

- Next, when a vowel does not follow the letters B, C, D, G, H, P, Q, T, and Z, they are pronounced with a short *e*, like "eh," following them. Thus B is pronounced "beh," C is "seh," and so on. The letter Q is "queh," and V, when it appears next to a vowel, is "veh." If a vowel comes after one of these letters, pronounce the letter as in English.

- When a vowel does not come after them, the letters K, L, R, W, and Y are pronounced with a long *a*, like "ah," following them. Thus K is pronounced "kah," L is "la," and so on. If a vowel comes after one of these letters, pronounce it as in English.

- When a vowel does not come before them, the letters F, M, N, S, and X are pronounced with a short *e*, like "eh," in front of them. Thus F is pronounced "eff," M is "em," and so on. The letter X is pronounced "ets." If a vowel comes before one of these letters, pronounce it as in English.

- Using this system, the name TLBR is pronounced Telabirah, the name AMDN is pronounced Amden, the name ROWB is pronounced Rowabeh, and the name KGYZ is pronounced Kageyazeh. Where you place the stress and accent is up to you, since the pronunciation is simply a convenience. The name is a constellation of energies, and speaking it aloud is simply a way of bringing those energies into focus in your consciousness.

- If you prefer to work with Judeo-Christian symbolism, it is traditional to add the syllable "el" or "iel" to the end of the name of your genius or any beneficial spirit to identify it as a spirit of God. In this case the four names just given would be pronounced Telabirahel, Amdeniel, Rowabeyel, and Kageyazel. If you prefer to work with Pagan symbolism, of course, this step is unnecessary.

Invoking Your Guardian Genius

Once you have determined the ruling planet and magical name of your guardian genius, the final step awaits you—invoking your genius and receiving its knowledge and conversation. This is often a slow process, calling for plenty of time and many repetitions, because it requires you to turn your awareness from the corpus mundi to the anima mundi and experience the spiritual dimension of the world directly. Like anything else worth doing, it takes work.

You can choose from among a wide range of practical methods for this work. One of the most common approaches to contacting the genius in Renaissance magic, for example, was ordinary prayer. To follow this path, you might pray daily to whatever spiritual power or powers you worship, asking him, her, or them to bring you into contact with your genius. You can pray spontaneously, if you prefer, or work out a prayer and repeat it every time you pray. Such a prayer is particularly worthwhile just before you cast your daily geomantic chart.

Meditation and scrying, using the methods outlined in Chapter Eight, is another tried and true way to contact your genius. Start by meditating on the planet that rules your genius, and try to explore the ways the influence of that planet affects your life. When you feel you have learned as much about this as you can, go on to meditate on the four figures in the cardines of the chart you cast to find the name of your genius. The figure in the first house expresses the personality of your genius, the figure in the tenth the spiritual powers that work through it, the figure in the seventh the special gifts it brings to you, and the figure in the fourth the results you can achieve through working with your genius.

After you have done this, do a scrying using the figure that was in the eleventh house of the chart that you cast to find the ruling planet of your genius. Once in the imaginal realm, call your genius by its name and ask it to come to you and speak with you. The results, like any scrying, will include some material from your own thoughts and some material from the mental chatter of the world around you, but within a short time flickers of communication with the genius begin to come through. As with any other scrying, use meditation to explore whatever you receive, and remember that self-deception is always a possibility in this form of work.

Finally, contemplative or theurgic ritual can be used to make contact with your genius. Like the other methods, a ritual invocation will likely have to be repeated many times before you enter into full conscious communion with your genius. You can craft your own ritual for this, using any magical system you prefer. Alternatively, you can use the ritual methods already given in this chapter.

If you prefer the second option, choose an hour governed by the geomantic figure that corresponds to your genius, on a day governed by the ruling planet of the figure, when the Moon is waxing. Set up your ritual space as you would for any other geomantic ritual, with the chair in the west facing east. Before the hour of the figure, take a purifying bath, don your ritual garments, and enter the ritual space as the hour begins.

Open the ritual using either the contemplative or the theurgic method. Burn incense appropriate to the ruling planet of the day and figure. Recite the Orphic Hymn to the genius or the prayer to the genius from the *Arbatel of Magic* in the appendix, or some other prayer or invocation that seems appropriate to you. Once you have done this, if you prefer the contemplative method, take your seat in the chair and meditate on your genius. If you prefer the theurgic method, invoke your genius in your own words, asking it to appear to you. In either case, when it seems appropriate, become silent, and wait for an answer. If none comes, wait longer, and then finally close using the appropriate method.

It often takes many such attempts before your genius appears. Long before you achieve the knowledge and conversation of your genius, however, you can expect sudden glimpses, insights, and intuitions to surface in your mind. These "tremblings of the veil" are messages from your genius. As you continue with the work of invocation, they will become more and more common, as your awareness opens to the inner side of things and you gradually awaken to this highest dimension of the geomancer's path.

INVOCATIONS FOR GEOMANTIC MAGIC

The Orphic Hymns

Among the most important works of religious poetry from ancient Greece, the Orphic hymns were written sometime before the sixth century BCE, supposedly by Orpheus, the mythic poet-singer and founder of the Greek mysteries. There are more than sixty of them, and they invoke most of the gods, goddesses, and powers of ancient Greek religion. Like most of the religious lore of the classical world, they were lost to the Christian West after the fall of Rome, but recovered from Byzantium in the early Renaissance.

Almost immediately after their rediscovery they became a core resource of Renaissance magic. The great mage Marsilio Ficino, whose translations of Hermetic texts kickstarted the Renaissance revival of occultism, used to sing the Orphic hymns to tunes of his own composition, accompanying himself on the *lira da bracchio* (an ancestor of the violin), to conjure down the powers of the planets.

Modern geomancers who prefer to use the names of Pagan gods and goddesses in their rituals will find that they make excellent invocations. I have included the hymns to the gods and goddesses of the seven planets, along with the hymn to the genius, which expresses powerfully the reverence classical Pagans felt toward their guardian spirits. The translation of the hymns given here is by the great eighteenth-century Platonist Thomas Taylor, updated to account for changes in the English language since Taylor's time.

The Orphic Hymn to Saturn

Ethereal father, mighty Titan, hear,
Great sire of Gods and men, whom all revere:
Endued with various council, pure and strong,
To whom perfection and decrease belong.
Consumed by thee all forms that hourly die,
By thee restored, their former place supply;
The world immense in everlasting chains,
Strong and ineffable thy power contains.
Father of vast eternity, divine,
O mighty Saturn, various speech is thine:
Blossom of Earth and of the starry skies,
Husband of Rhea, and Prometheus wise.
Productive Nature, venerable root,
From which the various forms of being shoot;
No parts peculiar can thy power enclose,
Diffused through all, from which the world arose,
O, best of beings, of a subtle mind,
Propitious hear to holy prayers inclined;
The sacred rites benevolent attend,
And grant a blameless life, a blessed end.

The Orphic Hymn to Jupiter

O Jove much-honored, Jove supremely great,
To thee our holy rites we consecrate,
Our prayers and expiations, king divine,
For all things round thy head exalted shine.
The Earth is thine, and mountains swelling high,
The sea profound, and all within the sky.
Great son of Saturn, descending from above,

Magnanimous, commanding, sceptred Jove;
All-parent, principle, and end of all,
Whose power almighty shakes this earthly ball;
Great Nature trembles at thy mighty nod,
Loud-sounding, armed with lightning, thundering God.
Source of abundance, purifying king,
O various-formed from whom all natures spring;
Propitious hear my prayer, give blameless health,
With peace divine, and necessary wealth.

The Orphic Hymn to Mars

Magnanimous, unconquered, boisterous Mars,
In arms rejoicing, and in bloody wars
Fierce and untamed, whose mighty power can make
The strongest walls from their foundations shake:
Mortal-destroying king, besmirched with gore,
Pleased with war's dreadful and tumultuous roar:
Thee, human blood and swords and spears delight,
And the dire ruin of mad savage fight.
Stay furious contests, and avenging strife,
Whose works with woe embitter human life;
To lovely Venus, and to Bacchus yield,
To Ceres give the weapons of the field;
Encourage peace, to gentle works inclin'd,
And give abundance, with benignant mind.

The Orphic Hymn to the Sun

Hear, golden Titan, whose eternal eye
With broad survey, illumines all the sky.

Self-born, unwearied in diffusing light,
And to all eyes the mirror of delight:
Lord of the seasons, with thy fiery car
And leaping coursers, beaming light from far:
With thy right hand the source of morning light,
And with thy left the father of the night.
Agile and vigorous, venerable Sun,
Fiery and bright around the skies you run.
Foe to the wicked, but the good man's guide,
O'er all his steps propitious you preside:
With various sounding, golden lyre, 'tis thine
To fill the world with harmony divine.
Father of ages, guide of prosperous deeds,
The world's commander, borne by lucid steeds,
Immortal Jove, all-searching, bearing light,
Source of existence, pure and fiery bright
Bearer of fruit, almighty lord of years,
Nimble and warm, whom every power reveres.
Great eye of Nature and the starry skies,
Bound with immortal flames to set and rise
Dispensing justice, lover of the stream,
The world's great master, and over all supreme.
Faithful defender, and the eye of right,
Of steeds the ruler, and of life the light:
With founding whip four fiery steeds you guide,
When in the car of day you glorious ride.
Propitious on these mystic labours shine,
And bless thy suppliants with a life divine.

The Orphic Hymn to Venus

Heavenly, illustrious, laughter-loving queen,
Sea-born, night-loving, of an awful mien;
Crafty, from whom necessity first came,
Producing, nightly, all-connecting dame:
'Tis thine the world with harmony to join,
For all things spring from thee, O power divine.
The triple Fates are ruled by thy decree,
And all productions yield alike to thee:
All that the heavens, encircling all, contain,
Earth fruit-producing, and the stormy main,
Thy sway confesses, and obeys thy nod,
Awful attendant of the wintry God:
Goddess of marriage, charming to the sight,
Mother of Loves, whom banquetings delight;
Source of persuasion, secret, favoring queen,
Illustrious born, apparent and unseen:
Spousal, lupercal, and to men inclined,
Prolific, most-desired, life-giving, kind:
Great sceptre-bearer of the Gods, 'tis thine,
Mortals in necessary bands to join;
And every tribe of savage monsters dire
In magic chains to bind, through mad desire.
Come, Cyprus-born, and to my prayer incline,
Whether exalted in the heavens you shine,
Or pleased in Syria's temple to preside,
Or o'er Egyptian plains thy car to guide,
Fashioned of gold; and near its sacred flood,
Fertile and famed to fix thy blest abode;
Or if rejoicing in the azure shores,
Near where the sea with foaming billows roars,
The circling choirs of mortals, thy delight,

Or beauteous nymphs, with eyes cerulean bright,
Pleased by the dusty banks renowned of old,
To drive thy rapid, two-yoked car of gold;
Or if in Cyprus with thy mother fair,
Where married women praise thee every year,
And lovely virgins in the chorus join,
Adonis pure to sing and thee divine;
Come, all-attractive to my prayer inclined,
For thee, I call, with holy, reverent mind.

The Orphic Hymn to Mercury

Hermes, draw near, and to my prayer incline,
Angel of Jove, and Maia's son divine;
Studious of contests, ruler of mankind,
With heart almighty, and a prudent mind.
Celestial messenger, of various skill,
Whose powerful arts did watchful Argus kill:
With winged feet, 'tis thine through air to course,
O friend of man, and prophet of discourse:
Great life-supporter, to rejoice is thine,
In arts gymnastic, and in fraud divine:
With power endued all language to explain,
Of care the loosener, and the source of gain.
Whose hand contains of blameless peace the rod,
Corucian, blessed, profitable God;
Of various speech, whose aid in works we find,
And in necessities to mortals kind:
Dire weapon of the tongue, which men revere,
Be present, Hermes, and thy suppliant hear;
Assist my works, conclude my life with peace,
Give graceful speech, and memory's increase.

The Orphic Hymn to the Moon

Hear, Goddess queen, diffusing silver light,
Bull-horned and wandering through the gloom of Night.
With stars surrounded, and with circuit wide
Night's torch extending, through the heavens you ride:
Female and Male with borrowed rays you shine,
And now full-orbed, now tending to decline.
Mother of ages, fruit-producing Moon,
Whose amber orb makes Night's reflected noon:
Lover of horses, splendid, queen of Night,
All-seeing power bedecked with starry light.
Lover of vigilance, the foe of strife,
In peace rejoicing, and a prudent life:
Fair lamp of Night, its ornament and friend,
Who gives to Nature's works their destined end.
Queen of the stars, all-wife Diana hail!
Decked with a graceful robe and shining veil;
Come, blessed Goddess, prudent, starry, bright,
Come lunar lamp with chaste and splendid light,
Shine on these sacred rites with prosperous rays,
And pleased, accept thy suppliant's mystic praise.

The Orphic Hymn to the Genius

Thee, mighty-ruling, Genius great, I call,
Mild Jove,* life-giving, and the source of all:
Great Jove,* much-wandering, terrible and strong,
To whom revenge and tortures dire belong.
Mankind from thee, in plenteous wealth abound,
When in their dwellings joyful thou art found;
Or pass through life afflicted and distressed,

The needful means of bliss by thee suppressed.
'Tis thine alone endued with boundless might,
To keep the keys of sorrow and delight.
O holy, blessed parent, hear my prayer,
Disperse the seeds of life-consuming care;
With favoring mind the sacred rites attend,
And grant my days a glorious, blessed end.

*Women using this hymn should replace the name "Jove" with "Juno" here, since guardian spirits share the gender of the person they protect. The names "Jove" and "Juno" were used as titles of the genius in classical times, because the genius ruled over the individual the way that, in Roman belief, Jove and Juno ruled over the cosmos.

The Heptameron Conjurations

Geomancers who prefer to use the divine and angelic names from the Judeo-Christian tradition, either because their own religious faith comes from that tradition, or because they practice another system of magic derived from it, may use any set of planetary invocations suited to their taste. Among the most widely used and respected conjurations are those first published by Pietro d'Abano, the famous fourteenth–century geomancer and mage, in his book *Heptameron*.

I have translated these conjurations into English below. Those who prefer to use the Latin originals will find them in the widely available *Fourth Book of Occult Philosophy* credited to Henry Cornelius Agrippa. I have also added a prayer for the invocation of the genius from the *Arbatel of Magic*, another magical text included with the *Fourth Book*.

The Conjuration of Saturn

I conjure and command you, Cassiel, Machatori, and Seraquiel, strong and powerful angels, and by the name Adonai, Adonai, Adonai, Eie, Eie, Eie, Acim, Acim, Acim, Cados, Cados, Ima, Ima, Ima, Saclai, Ia, Sar, the Lord who establishes the ages, who rested on the seventh day; and by Him who in His good pleasure gave the children of Israel His Law as an inheritance, that they might firmly keep it, and be blessed by it, that they might thereby receive in another age a blessed reward; and by the names of the angels who serve in the seventh host in the presence of the angel Pooel, the powerful prince; and by the name of thy star, which is Saturn; and by its holy seal; and by the aforesaid names, I conjure thee, thou great angel Cassiel, who art set over Saturn, that you will perform all these things according to my will and desire.

The Conjuration of Jupiter

I conjure and command you, holy angels, by the name Cados, Cados, Cados, Escherie, Escherie, Escherie Hatimya, mighty establisher of the ages, Cantine, Iaim, Ianic, Anic, Calbat, Sabbac, Berifay, Alnaym; and by the name of Adonai, who created fishes and creeping things in the water, and birds above the face of the Earth, flying toward the heavens on the fifth day; and by the names of the angels who serve in the sixth host in the presence of the angel Pastore, the holy, great, and powerful prince; and by the name of thy star, which is Jupiter; and by the name of its seal; and by the name of Adonai, the highest God, and creator of all things; and by the name of all the stars, and by their power and virtue; and by the aforesaid names, I conjure thee, thou great angel Sachiel, who art set over Jupiter, that you will perform all these things according to my will and desire.

The Conjuration of the Mars

I conjure and command thee, strong and holy angels, by the names Ia, Ia, Ia, He, He, He, Hi, Hi, Hi, Ha, Ha, Ha, Va, Va, Va, An, An, An, Aie, Aie, Aie, El, Ai, Elibra, Eloim, Eloim, and by the names of the same high God, who made dry land appear from the waters, and called it Earth, and produced trees and herbs from it, and sealed it with his precious, honorable, terrible and holy name; and by the names of the angels commanded in the fifth host, who serve the great, strong, powerful and honored angel Acimoy; and by the name of thy star, which is Mars; and by the aforesaid names, I conjure thee, thou great angel Samael, who art set over Mars; and by name of Adonai, the living and true God, that you will perform all these things according to my will and desire.

The Conjuration of the Sun

I conjure and command thee, strong and holy angels of God, in the names Adonai, Eie, Eie, Eie, who is and was and shall be, Eie, Abraye; and in the names Sadai, Cados, Cados, Cados, whose wings spread above the Cherubim, and by the great name of the same God who is strong and mighty, and is exalted over every heaven, Eie, Saraie, who establishes the ages, who created the universe, the heavens, the Earth, the sea, and all that are in them on the first day, and sealed them with his holy name Phaa; and by the name of the holy angels commanded in the fourth host, who serve in the presence of the mighty Salamia, the great and honored angel, and by the name of thy star, which is the Sun, and by its sign, and by the immeasurable name of the living God, and by all the aforesaid names, I conjure thee, Michael, thou great angel, who art set over the Sun; and by the name of Adonai, the God of Israel, who created the world and all that is in it, that you will perform all these things according to my will and desire.

The Conjuration of Venus

I conjure and command you, strong, holy, and powerful angels, by the name On, Hei, Heia, Ia, Ie, Adonai, Sadai; and by the name of Sadai, who created four-footed beasts and crawling animals and human beings in the sixth day, and to Adam gave power over all animals; whence the blessed name of the creator is in his place; and by the names of the angels who serve in the third host in the presence of the great angel Dagiel, the strong and powerful prince; and by the name of thy star, which is Venus; and by the name of its seal, which is most holy; and by the aforesaid names, I conjure thee, thou great angel Anael, who art set over Venus, that you will perform all these things according to my will and desire.

The Conjuration of Mercury

I conjure and command thee, strong, holy, and powerful angels, in the strong, most terrible and blessed names Ia, Adonai, Eloim, Sadai, Sadai, Sadai, Eie, Eie, Eie, Asamie, Asaraie, and in the name of Adonai, the God of Israel, who created the great lights, and distinguished day from night; and by the name of all the angels who serve in the second host in the presence of the great, strong, and potent angel Tetra; and by the name of thy star, which is Mercury, and by the name of the seal, which was sealed by the most strong and honored God; by all the aforesaid I conjure thee, thou great angel Raphael, who is set over

Mercury; and by the holy name of the most holy Creator that was written upon the brow of the high priest Aaron; and by the names of the angels who are strengthened by the grace of the Savior, and by the name of the thrones of the Holy Living Creatures that have six wings, that you will perform all these things according to my will and desire.

The Conjuration of the Moon

I conjure and command thee, strong and beneficent angels, in the names Adonai, Adonai, Adonai, Eie, Eie, Eie, Cados, Cados, Cados, Achim, Achim, Ia, Ia, the strong, Ia, who appeared on Mount Sinai, for the glorification of the king Adonai, Sadai, Zebaoth, Anathai, Ia, Ia, Ia, Marinata, Abim, Ieia, who made the salt sea and all waters on the second day, those above the heavens as well as those on Earth; and sealed the sea in his exalted name, and the boundaries which he has established, it shall not exceed; and by the name of the angels who are commanded in the first host, who serve the great angel Orphaniel, precious and honored, and by the name of thy star, which is the Moon, and by the names aforesair, I conjure thee, Gabriel, who art set over the Moon, that you will perform all these things according to my will and desire.

Prayer to Invoke the Genius

O Lord of heaven and Earth, creator and maker of all things visible and invisible, I, though unworthy, by Thy assistance call upon Thee,* that thou wilt give unto me Thy holy spirit, to direct me in Thy truth unto all good. Amen.

Because I earnestly desire perfectly to know the arts of this life, and such things as are necessary for us, who are so overwhelmed in darkness, and polluted with infinite human opinions, that I of my own power can attain to no knowledge in them, unless Thou teach it me: grant me therefore one of Thy spirits, who may teach me those things which Thou wouldst have me to know and learn, to Thy praise and glory, and the profit of our neighbor. Give me also an apt and teachable heart, that I may easily understand those things which Thou shalt teach me, and may hide them in my understanding, that I may bring them forth as out of Thy inexhaustible treasures, to all necessary uses. And give me grace, that I may use such Thy gifts humbly, with fear and trembling,* with Thy holy spirit. Amen.

*Christian geomancers may choose to insert the words "through Jesus Christ our Lord" at the points marked with asterisks.

BIBLIOGRAPHY

Abano, Pietro d'. *Modo Judicandi Questiones Secundum Petrum de Abano Patavinum*. In Charmasson, *Recherches sur une Technique Divinatoire: La Geomancie dans l'Occident Medieval*. Geneva: Librairie Droz, 1980.

Agrippa, Henry Cornelius (pseud.). *On Geomancy, in Fourth Book of Occult Philosophy*. Repr. Kila, MT: Kessinger, 1992.

————. *Three Books of Occult Philosophy,* trans. James Freake, ed. Donald Tyson. St. Paul: Llewellyn, 1993.

Agrippa, Henry Cornelius (pseud.). *Fourth Book of Occult Philosophy.* Repr. Kila, MT: Kessinger, 1992.

Alighieri, Dante. *The Divine Comedy,* trans. H. F. Cary. NY: Collier, 1909.

Anonymous (ed.). *Fasciculus Geomanticus.* Verona: n.p., 1704.

Bascom, William. *Ifa Divination: Communication Between Gods and Men in West Africa.* Bloomington: Indiana UP, 1969.

Case, John. *The Angelical Guide.* London: Isaac Dawkins, 1697.

Cattan, Christopher. *The Geomancy of Master Christopher Cattan.* London: John Wolf, 1591; reprinted n.p.: Antiquus Astrologia, 2007.

Charmasson, Therese. *Recherches sur une Technique Divinatoire: La Geomancie dans l'Occident Medieval.* Geneva: Librairie Droz, 1980.

Cicero, Chic, and Sandra Tabatha Cicero. *Secrets of a Golden Dawn Temple.* St. Paul, MN: Llewellyn, 1992.

Ficino, Marsilio. *Three Books on Life,* tr. Carol V. Kaske and John R. Clark. Tempe, AZ: MRTS, 2002.

Fludd, Robert. *De Geomantia,* in *Fasciculus Geomanticus,* edited by Anonymous. Verona: n.p., 1704.

————. *De intellectualis scientia, seu Geomantia.* In *Fasciculus Geomanticus,* edited by Anonymous. Verona: n.p., 1704.

————. *Traité de Géomancie,* trans. P.-V. Piobb. Paris: Éditions Dangles, 1947.

Heninger, S. K., Jr. *Touches of Sweet Harmony: Pythagorean Cosmology and Renaissance Poetics.* San Marino, CA: Huntington Library, 1974.

Heydon, John. *Theomagia, or the Temple of Wisdome.* London: for Henry Brome at the Gun in Ivie-Lane, and for Thomas Rooks at the Lambe at the east end of St. Pauls, 1664.

Hulse, David Allen. *The Key Of It All, Book Two: The Western Mysteries.* St. Paul: Llewellyn, 1994.

I Ching or Book of Changes, The, trans. Richard Wilhelm and Cary F. Baynes. Princeton: Princeton University Press, 1967.

Jaulin, Robert. *La Geomancie: Analyse Formelle.* Paris: Mouton, 1966.

Josten, C. H. "Robert Fludd's Theory of Geomancy and his Experiences at Avignon in the Winter of 1601 to 1602." *Journal of the Warburg and Courtauld Institutes* 27 (1964), 327–35.

King, Francis, and Stephen Skinner. *Techniques of High Magic.* New York: Avon, 1976.

Layne, Meade. *The Art of Geomancy.* Bayside, CA: Borderland Sciences, n.d.

Lessa, William A. "Divining Knots in the Carolines." *Journal of the Polynesian Society* 68 (1959), 188–204.

McLean, Adam, ed. *The Magical Calendar.* Grand Rapids, MI: Phanes, 1994.

Pennick, Nigel. *Games of the Gods.* York Beach, ME: Weiser, 1989.

————. *The Oracle of Geomancy.* Chievely, Berks: Capall Bann, 1995.

Regardie, Israel. *The Complete Golden Dawn System of Magic.* Phoenix: Falcon, 1984.

————. *A Practical Guide to Geomantic Divination.* NY: Samuel Weiser, 1972.

————. *The Golden Dawn.* St. Paul: Llewellyn, 1971.

Schwei, Priscilla, and Ralph Pestka. *The Complete Book of Astrological Geomancy.* St. Paul: Llewellyn, 1990.

Skinner, Stephen. *The Oracle of Geomancy.* Bridport, Dorset: Prism, 1986.

————. *Terrestrial Astrology.* London: Routledge & Kegan Paul, 1980.

Westcott, William Wynn, ed. *The Chaldean Oracles of Zoroaster.* Wellingborough, UK: Aquarian, 1983.

INDEX

meditation, 77, 171–180
metoscopy, 22
modes of perfection, 114–122
multiple significators, 135–139
mutation, 117–118

natura naturans, 27
natura naturata, 26

occupation, 115
Orphic hymns, 231–238

Padua, 15
Paganism, 213
palmistry, 21–22
part of fortune, 128
Pietro di Abano, 16–17, 20, 208, 213, 238
projection of points, 128

reconciler, 127

scientific revolution, 20
scrying, 180–186
shield chart, 82, 87–99
sigils, geomantic, 193–196
Smith, Pamela Coleman, 172
special questions, 153–166
spirits, geomantic, 78–81, 215–218
spiritus mundi, 27, 78, 181–182

ABOUT THE AUTHOR

John Michael Greer has been a student of the occult traditions for more than 25 years. The current Grand Archdruid of the Ancient Order of Druids in America (AODA), he is also a longtime Golden Dawn initiate, a geomancer and a student of sacred geometry. Greer is the author of numerous articles and eighteen books, including *The Druidry Handbook, The Druid Magic Handbook,* and *The Long Descent: A User's Guide to the End of the Industrial Age*. He is also the co-author of *Learning Ritual Magic* and *Pagan Prayer Beads*. He lives in Ashland, Oregon with his wife Sara.

© Patrick Claflin

TO OUR READERS

Weiser Books, an imprint of Red Wheel/Weiser, publishes books across the entire spectrum of occult and esoteric subjects. Our mission is to publish quality books that will make a difference in people's lives without advocating any one particular path or field of study. We value the integrity, originality, and depth of knowledge of our authors.

Our readers are our most important resource, and we appreciate your input, suggestions, and ideas about what you would like to see published. Please feel free to contact us, to request our latest book catalog, or to be added to our mailing list.

Red Wheel/Weiser, LLC
500 Third Street, Suite 230
San Francisco, CA 94107
www.redwheelweiser.com